CONTEN

PREFACE

ABOUT 12 YEARS ago I stopped working and decided to make a million pounds instead. Simple as that!

Well, that's not strictly true. What really happened is that I stopped working (which never really suited me if I'm honest) and decided that...well, I'd sort of like to make some money doing... erm... something else. In my own mind I had a figure of a quarter of a million pounds which seemed like a fantastic sum. If I could make that I'd be satisfied. Now all I needed to do was come up with a way to do it. How naive and unfocused can you get?

For a long time, even a quarter of a million pounds looked like a pipe dream. Hardly surprising given that I was starting from scratch, with few marketable skills visible to the naked eye, and with little or no idea of what I was going to do.

I tried out a few things, read a few books, took a few courses, and somehow managed to make enough money to replace what I was previously earning. Great. But my bank account told the real story. I was pretty much at the same stage as when I started. Slightly better than broke - but not much.

It's at this point in most 'rags to riches' stories that you hear about a single blinding flash of inspiration, chance meeting, or fantastic discovery which turned the tide over night. Sorry, but life isn't like that. Or at least mine isn't. Over a period of a couple of years, I experimented with a number of ideas, techniques and strategies I'd either read about or seen other people using, weeded out the ones that didn't work and embraced the ones that did. I added a few 'twists' to the techniques I'd learned, and even developed a few of my own.

Trial and error works well. It just takes time. Bit by bit, things started to fall into place. As my original target of a quarter of a million pounds grew larger in my sights, I started to realise how pathetic it was. So I replaced it with an 'impossible' one - a million pounds!

I've spoken to a lot of people who've made a million or more from scratch, and they all tell you the same two things. When they set out, it seemed like an impossible dream, but when they reached the goal it didn't seem like a big deal. Nothing more than a stepping stone. Quite often, they pass the target without even noticing. And that's how it was for me, and how it's continued to be as each new target has been reached, and then left as little more than a dot in life's rear view mirror.

It's only when I force myself to take a detached view that I realise how far I've come, and that what doesn't seem like a 'bid deal' today would have seemed like a wild fantasy just a few short years ago. That's what gave me the confidence (some might say arrogance) to write this book.

The way I see it, if I can stop working and make a million pounds instead, anybody can. If I can do it without any special skills or start up capital, you can too. And if I tell you, before you start, what I learned along the way, you can do it a dammed site quicker than I did.

A word of warning though - I don't have all the answers. I can't tell you how to create a world beating original product. I've never done it. I can't tell you how to float your fledgling company on the stockmarket and pocket £20 million overnight. I wouldn't know where to start. I can't tell you how to prise £500,000 start-up capital out of the clutches of your bank or venture capitalists. I've never borrowed a penny in my life.

But what I can share with you (if you're interested) is the information, techniques, ideas and strategies I've learned in my own journey through stopping working and making a million pounds instead. As you read what follows, you might form the opinion that I'm saying that my approach is cast in stone - the only one that works. Well that's simply not true. If I appear a little dogmatic at times, it's because I'm sharing ideas which I know work - not because nothing else could.

I hope you find the book both interesting and informative and that it plays at least a small part in helping you achieve your own money making goals - whatever they might be.

JOHN HARRISON - STREETWISE MARKETING

INTRODUCTION

A CYNIC MIGHT argue that only the greedy, the lazy or the foolish would buy a book entitled *How to Stop Working And Make A Million Pounds Instead*. Greedy because £1 million is a huge sum of money, lazy because they don't want to work for it, and foolish because it's an impossible dream.

Well a cynic would be wrong... wrong... and wrong again!

I don't want to insult or offend you, (especially this early in the book - I'm saving that for later) but a million pounds isn't a fortune these days. It really isn't. With a million pounds in the bank, you've taken the very first small step on the wealth ladder. At the last count, well over 100,000 people in the UK had taken that step. So if it's an impossible dream, there are going to be an awful lot of disappointed people about to wake up in a cold sweat any day soon.

So making your million is attainable. Ordinary people are doing it every day. People like you. The only difference between you and them is that they worked out a way to do it and then followed it through. In this book, I'm going to help you do that too.

Twenty or 30 years ago a million pounds was a serious sum of money. You really could live like a millionaire. Now? Buy yourself a decent house, a nice car, and what's left will return you about the same as the head of Geography earns in your local comprehensive. Hardly champagne, caviar and international jet setting, now is it? However, it might not earn you more than the aforementioned Geography teacher, although you won't have to run the gauntlet of a constant stream of juvenile delinquents to get it.

A million pounds puts you into the category that the middle classes have always euphemistically called 'comfortable.' There's a lot to be said for knowing that whatever happens, there will always be a roof over your head, food on the table, clothes on your families back, a car in the garage, and a few extra quid left over for a couple of holidays in the sun every year. And that's whether you decide to work or not.

When you get right down to it, you don't need any more than this. In fact you don't really need all of it. Knowing that you will always have it though - whatever happens - is extremely reassuring, and frees your mind up for the challenge ahead - if you choose to accept it...

Making Some Real Money!

Most experts agree that in order to 'live like a millionaire' these days, you need somewhere between £5-10 million. With that kind of money, you have a passive income (one you don't have to work for) of around £10,000 a week. That's real money - still a long way away from the Premier League, but somewhere in the middle of Division One.

The £500 a week or so you're going to earn from the residue of your million is nice. It will keep the 'wolf from the door,' but it's not real wealth. But it is a start, and the first million is always the most difficult to make.

I'm not telling you any of this at the outset to discourage or dissuade you, but merely to dispel the notion that a million pounds is a massive sum of money, and therefore beyond the reach of the average man or woman. It's a sum which has taken on mythical status. Time and inflation now give lie to the myth.

When I was a kid, my response to the question, *"What do you want to be when you grow up?"* was always the same... *"I want to be a millionaire."* Did I succeed? Well the answer is *"yes,"* and *"not yet."* If you've followed my opening ramblings you'll know exactly what I mean, and why when I say what I do, it's with the benefit of experience and hindsight.

So I hope you're with me when I say that aiming to make a million is neither greedy nor over-ambitious. It is, if anything, a fairly cautious goal, and the bare minimum you should be aiming for if you're contemplating embarking on a wealth building exercise. Any money making programme is going to involve a degree of time, effort and sacrifice on your part (more on that later!), and it's crucial that the ratio of effort to reward is in your favour if you're to do what's necessary to succeed. In other words, it has to be worth the price.

I sense some furrowed brows and uneasy shuffling at this point. I think it was the mention of time, effort and sacrifice that did it; that and the fact that this book is called *How To Stop Working And Make A Million Pounds Instead*.

Let me explain. I don't think, unless you are really lucky, that you can make a million pounds or more if you continue to work. And I mean that on two levels.

If you sell your labour to the highest bidder (work for someone else) it's very unlikely that you will ever accumulate a meaningful amount of money. I know you can probably recount examples of people who have made money in this way - top company directors, city high flyers and the like - but they are very much the exception.

There are a number of reasons why you're unlikely to accumulate real wealth as a paid employee, and we'll be looking at this in detail later, but for now, just consider the following:

Even if you earn £100,000 a year with an employer, (and how many people do that?) and you spend a very modest £20,000 a year to live, after taking taxes into account, you're unlikely to save more than £40,000 a year. At that rate, it's going to take you about 25 years of very frugal, miserable, penny-pinching living to amass your million. What's the point in that?

I've simplified things a little, but hopefully you get the message. You won't make your million working for someone else. The clear implication therefore, is that you're going to have to make your money from your own businesses, schemes or projects.

I've just checked my dictionary, and under the entry for 'work,' I found the words 'toil' and 'labour.' That brings me to the second reason you must stop working if you're ever to make your million...and a confession!

For a number of years now I have been harbouring a guilty secret - something that I knew if it ever got out, would expose me to ridicule from just about everyone I know. At first, I tried to dismiss it as a passing phase. Just one of those things that you grow out of. After all, I never used to feel like this. Go back 12 years or so, and I used to be like everyone else. I used to be normal.

But I've given it long enough, I have to concede that it's not going away. I'm just going to have to learn to live with it, and the first stage in that process is to come clean and tell the world (or at least the small part of it reading this), and hope people will accept me for what I am. So here it is - my confession... I like Monday mornings!

There, I've said it! That wasn't so bad after all! And it's true. I actually like Monday mornings - it represents the start of a new working week and all the potential opportunities it will bring. Great!

At first, I thought I was alone, and then I started to hear about other people who felt the same way. I felt better! And I felt even better still when I figured out what these people all had in common... they were all extraordinarily successful.

You see, genuinely successful people don't ever suffer from what most people know as 'that Monday morning feeling.' They might pretend that they do - but they don't! And that's why they're high achievers - because they enjoy what they do.

Butch Stewart, founder of the Sandals resort chain, puts it this way:

"I honestly don't think I've worked a day in my life. To get paid to do all the things you like so much. There's no question about it: if you like what you are doing, then you have a focus about something, and you have a feel for it."

To make a great deal of money, (a million isn't a fortune, but it is a great deal by most peoples standards) it's important that you enjoy what you're doing. The great majority of wealthy people make their money doing things they absolutely love to do. They'd do it for nothing. Free! They continue to do it, long after the economic necessity has past; long after they could retire and go and play golf, lay in the sun, or do absolutely anything else their hearts desired.

They wouldn't associate the words 'toil' or 'labour' with what they do at all. They don't see it as 'work,' and if you're to achieve extra-ordinary financial success yourself then you're going to have to stop working and start doing something you love too.

When you feel like that, then Monday morning - in fact any morning - is a breeze. Instead of waking to a feeling of foreboding, people who have found their niche start the week with feelings of anticipation and enthusiasm for the opportunities which will present themselves in the days to come. It's this enthusiasm and the resultant positive actions it brings about which create great success.

Underachievers often console themselves with the fact that high achievers appear to be working much longer and harder for their rewards, and to a certain extent that's true. But here's the rub - while the under-achiever sees longer and harder work as a negative factor, the high achiever sees it as a positive one. Although he's working long and hard, he's having fun. And making money. He'd rather be doing that than anything else. That's the difference between being in the right job or business, and being in the wrong one. It's the difference between doing what you want to do, and doing what you have to do.

Give a little thought to how you feel on Monday mornings. It's an almost perfect barometer for whether you're on the right road, and whether that road is likely to lead to great success for you.

If you're on the wrong road, you've already taken the first step to do something about it by reading this book. No matter how far you've travelled, it's never too late to take a different route. This might involve losing a little ground in the short term, but once you get on the right track for you, the surface will be smoother, the traffic lighter, and you'll make far faster progress as a result.

By reading this book you are not showing yourself to be greedy, lazy or foolish. Rather, you are recognising a million pounds as a fairly modest, and perfectly attainable goal, and accepting the undisputable truth of the matter - that to get there, you're going to have to stop working and start doing something else instead. But what?

In the last two chapters of the book, I'm going to give you some ideas for what that something else could, and should, be...the businesses, systems and projects which give the average person without specialist skills or capital, the maximum chance of fulfilling that million pound dream. But we're not ready for that yet. To take up any of these ideas at this stage would be like building a house on quicksand. You need firm foundations to build a house, and likewise, you need firm foundations to build your own money making machine - one which will pass the test of time.

These foundations are the perceptions, attitudes, ideas, knowledge and practices which you'll need to embrace and act upon if you're to succeed. In short, you're going to have to change the way you think, and this in turn will change the way you act, and as night follows day, this will change the results you get when you embark on one or more money making projects.

I can't over-emphasise how important this is. If you've set out with the goal of making a great deal of money in the past, and have not been successful, it may be because you set out with the 'wrong' business or project. But more likely, it's because you didn't have the foundations in place - the foundations that are routed firmly right inside your head.

Don't worry though. This isn't a book about self hypnosis, positive affirmations, meditation or any of 1,001 other psychological self improvement techniques. They can all be useful. They all have their place, but it isn't here. My goal is clear. It's to remove all the negative perceptions, attitudes, ideas and beliefs you may have unwittingly taken on board about the creation of personal wealth, and then to replace them with the positive wealth building thought processes you must have in place if you're to stop working and make a million pounds instead.

So, let's get started. In the opening section, we're going to explore why you deserve wealth, and why you owe it to yourself and your family to work towards it.

Until you truly believe that you deserve wealth and it's a worthwhile, ethical and attainable goal, it's impossible to move forward.

CHAPTER 1

Life - It's The Ultimate Money Game

LET'S BE HONEST and up-front about it, money is vitally important to all of us. Anyone who suggests otherwise has either taken a vow of poverty, accumulated vast quantities of the stuff and forgotten what it's like to have none, or they're a liar!

I think it safe to assume that someone reading a book entitled *How To Stop Working and Make a Million Pounds Instead* has more than a passing interest in making money, and what it can do. Irrespective of what they may tell you, almost everyone you come into contact with each day feels exactly the same way. They just have trouble admitting it.

Ask a random group of a hundred people if they want to be fabulously wealthy, and maybe ten per cent will say yes. The rest will make the right noises about 'money not being the most important thing in the world' and being 'content with what they have.'

But ask the same 100 people whether they enter the national lottery or football pools, and you'll find around 80 per cent admitting that they do. So why do all these people who apparently aren't interested in becoming rich, enter a competition, the sole purpose of which is to make them... erm... rich?

I think what these people can't admit (maybe even to themselves) is that they do want to be rich, but they don't want to put in the effort they know will be necessary to make it happen. They want it handed on a plate, but if there's a price to pay, they're not willing to pay it - and so they lie. They say they don't want to be rich. It's a lot easier than saying "Yes sir, I would like to be rich, but only if the money just lands in my lap without me doing anything more arduous than ticking off six numbers on a lottery ticket." What self respecting person can admit that - even to themselves?

So don't fall for any self righteous claptrap; don't feel bad because you want money for yourself and are prepared to act to make it happen. You're already several rungs up from the majority who want the money, but won't pay the price.

Money may not be the most important thing in the world... but it is the most important thing over which we can exert absolute control. You might not be able to force anyone to love you, and you could experience health problems despite your very best preventative efforts, but approach your money making activities in the right way and you will always have more than enough. It's completely down to you.

Having 'enough' money brings with it security, choice, and most important of all... personal freedom. I once read of a wealthy business-man who explained the appeal perfectly...

"I view life as a game. The more money you have the more parts of the game you're allowed to play."

Isn't that true? So many of the great things which life has to offer are reserved for those with money. If you don't have the cash, you can't have the fancy cars, the big houses, the yachts, the private planes, the luxury holidays, the fine art, the antique furniture, the Premiership football team... or whatever it is that lights your particular fire.

Perhaps acquisition of possessions doesn't interest you. Maybe that's not the part of the 'game' you want to play. Fine, but I would suggest that whatever you want from life (you do want something, don't you?) the accumulation of wealth will be a positive factor in helping you to get it.

Want to carry out voluntary work? You could devote so much more time to it if you became personally financially secure first, couldn't you? Want to spend more time with your family? One of the most precious things that money can buy is control of your own time, to do with as you please. You can't spend time with your family if you're working long hours for an employer just to keep your head above water.

Want to put something back into your local community or help out a charity? Once you've accumulated substantial wealth it's yours to do with as you please. Only the wealthy get to play the charitable giving part of the 'game' at the highest level. In order to give money you must first make money.

Do you follow the point I'm making? Whatever parts of the game of life you want to play, whether they be purely the acquisitive and self centred parts, or the more altruistic and outwardly focussed ones, your economic success will be the major determinant of the level at which you can play.

In other words, there is no excuse for failing to make the most of the money making opportunities which are available to you. Don't try to kid yourself that you don't need money for what you want out of life. Whatever you want, you can have it quicker, better or more of it with the right amount of money behind you.

Exploding the Big Money Myths

Some of the factors which might be temporarily holding you back from achieving your million pound goal are obvious. Things like a lack of capital, skills or knowledge will have at least some effect. Generally we can immediately recognise this, and take some positive action to do something about it. More about that later.

But there are other factors which are less obvious and tangible, and as a result are potentially more damaging. Why? Because if we don't know what's wrong, how can we go about fixing it?

The most damaging restrictions are those we don't know are there. That's because they take the form of ideas and beliefs, which if not questioned will affect our judgment, our attitude and our actions. There are so many of these negative ideas and perceptions about money, that it's hardly surprising that a lot of people are put off ever making any effort to acquire some for themselves.

Here are the most common money myths...

Myth No.1 - Money Can't Buy You Happiness

Of all the myths, "Money can't buy you happiness" is probably the most prevalent and the most damaging. It's widely accepted and rarely seriously questioned - mainly because it's true. But that's only part of the story.

The implication is that acquiring money will in some way bring misery. To prove their argument, the naysayers wheel out examples of rich people who do not appear to be full of the joys of spring. Ever seen a picture of John Paul Getty smiling? Me neither.

And then they show you a photograph of some poverty stricken Ethiopian, emerging from his mud hut with a huge beaming smile on his face. Case proven m'lud!

Not quite. Everyone has their own inherent and underlying level of happiness, independent of their economic status. Money won't make you happy, but it won't make you unhappy either. And enough of it will give you the opportunity to play any part of the game of life you desire. And if that doesn't make you happier, nothing will.

If all else fails, it's an undeniable fact that rich and miserable beats poor and miserable every time.

Myth No.2 - The Best Things In Life Are Free

Ever heard that one? Of course you have. Once again, there's an element of truth here which makes this all the more damaging. The implication is that because the most important things in life can't be bought, there's no point in striving for wealth.

A couple of years ago, I met a well known sports personality who has become a millionaire in recent years. And yet he has little interest in the things money can buy. For him, the great things in life are the things he gets for free - the love of his family, the satisfaction he gets from his work, and the opportunity to benefit from the wonders of the natural world. And yet paradoxically, the money itself was very important to him.

He explained it to me this way - *"It's my F**k Off money."* He knows that whatever happens, he'll never have to do anything he doesn't want to, he'll never have to work with anyone he doesn't choose to, and he'll never have to do anything against his principles - simply to put food on the table.

Possessing a substantial amount of money can buy you the freedom you desire - even if you have absolutely no interest in the material things it can bring.

Myth No.3 - Accumulating Money Is Morally Wrong

Another obstacle which holds many people back from striving for wealth is the moral dilemma. Accumulating a great stash of cash may be good for you, but is it right for some people to have so much, while others have so little. Is it just? Is it fair in a modern 'caring and sharing' society? It's an argument you'll need to settle firmly in your own mind if you're to carry through what's necessary to make your million.

Employment has seldom been less secure. Even previously 'safe' jobs in the Civil Service and Banking are disappearing at an alarming rate. State benefits are being eroded away too. It's very unlikely that anyone currently under the age of 40 will receive a state pension, for example. It seems to me that every responsible person should make independent provision for their own financial well being, whether they be employed, unemployed or self employed at the moment.

The concept of a 'caring and sharing' society is a very attractive one. But it has never existed, and sadly, it never will. It's a convenient media invention which flies in the face of basic human nature. If you fall on hard times, the only person you can rely on is you, and your immediate family - if you're lucky. Regrettably, no one else will either care... or share!

The wealthy have always realised this of course. Whatever the pre-vailing media inspired 'mood of the nation', they have continued to do what they have always done...accumulated as much money as possible, in as short a period as possible - and hung on to it.

Immoral? Well the wealthy are without doubt the biggest contributors to charities and other good causes. They are the greatest providers of general wealth, through the creation of employment which didn't previously exist. Individual wealth is rarely created without simultaneously creating wealth for others.

And the rich are also (with the exception of a few 'bad apples') the largest contributors to the coffers of the exchequer, which is precisely where the state benefits come from to look after the people who either can't or won't make provision for themselves. Think about it!

You need feel no guilt in making as much money as you possible can. By doing so, you are helping yourself, your family, the country...and yes, even the people who either choose or are forced to rely on others to provide for their welfare!

Myth No.4 - Profits Can Be Excessive

Consider the idea of 'excessive profits' for a moment. Do you think profits can really be excessive? A lot of politicians, journalists and other opinion leaders do, and you'll regularly see this adjective along with 'unfair' and 'obscene' preceding the word profit.

Anyone who truly believes that profits can be unfair, excessive or obscene is not going to do their best to earn this unsavoury amount of money. Why work hard to achieve something so negative?

The reality, of course, is that profits can never be excessive in a free market. If we charge too high a price for a product or service then the market will quickly tell us. It won't pay! So we have to reduce our price (and profit) or go out of business. It's as simple as that.

If you have a huge profit margin and the market is prepared to pay your price, then great. That isn't an obscene profit...it's a success! However, you can bet your bottom dollar that someone else will come into the market and undercut you, forcing you to reduce your prices and slash your profit margin in the process. That's how the free market works.

Outside monopoly industries, which are a different matter altogether, there's no such thing as excessive profit. So don't allow negativity about high profits to enter your thinking.

Myth No.5 - Some People Are Underpaid

Do you believe anyone is underpaid? Once again, many politicians, journalists and other opinion leaders do. That's why we're now all subject to minimum wage legislation, and why we have to endure article after article about how nurses should earn more money than they do.

If you buy into the 'underpaid' or 'slave wages' myth, then at least on a subconscious level, it makes it very difficult for you to be comfortable with the idea of employing people at an economic level. It also gives you a 'get out,' with respect to your own financial position, and who's responsible for it. We're going to talk about responsibility quite a bit, later.

We're all fortunate to live and work in a free labour market. If we don't like the terms and conditions of our employment, we have the option of voting with our feet. We can move to another job offering a salary more to our liking, start our own business... whatever we choose. Very simply, we can take our labour elsewhere.

In the same way that the free market for goods and services ensures that profits can never be excessive, the free labour market ensures that no-one can ever be underpaid. Any employer paying too little would have no employees. They would all defect to employers paying better wages. Our 'underpaying' employer would be forced to increase wages to stay in business.

That's precisely what happened a few years ago with respect to nurses' pay. It wasn't the newspapers bleating about the "poor underpaid nurses" that did the trick. It was simply market forces... too many nurses taking their labour elsewhere to get a better deal.

Now if we can't negotiate a better deal, can't find a better-paid job locally, aren't prepared to relocate to find one, or don't have the wherewithal to start our own profitable business, then the hard news is this: we're not underpaid. We are being paid exactly what we're worth in the marketplace.

We might not be paid as much as we'd like, or even as much as we can comfortably live on, but that's not the same thing. An employer doesn't have any responsibility whatsoever to pay us a penny more than we're worth in the marketplace, and if we're still working for them at the same rate of pay, that's what we're worth. It's our own individual responsibility to do something about it.

The danger of thinking otherwise though is this...if we believe we're underpaid and it's someone else's fault, then it removes all responsibility from our shoulders. It ensures that we'll do nothing positive about the situation. We'll just grumble that we're not being paid 'what we're worth,' and wait for the legislators to force someone to pay us more. Now they'll have to pay us the minimum wage... victory at last!

Breaking Down The Barriers

Money related myths like these can form invisible barriers to achieving what you want to achieve. I guarantee that you will have accepted many ideas like this, and they will be shaping your actions. Now might be a good time to critically examine all the ideas you've 'caught' from the media and the people around you without consciously realising it.

Do they all make sense? Does internalising them, and using them as a basis for action, enhance your chances of reaching your goals of stopping working and making a million pounds instead, or does it act to hold you back? Only you know, and only you can decide.

CHAPTER 2

Anyone and Everyone Can Do It - No More Excuses!

THE LATEST OFFICIAL figures show that there are over 100,000 millionaires in the UK, and the total number is growing. Many people would like to believe that the rich either inherited the money, won it, or acquired it by doing something 'dodgy' or some other effortless quirk of fate. They'd like to believe that because it absolves them of any responsibility for not achieving similar financial success.

I'm afraid they don't get off that lightly! A study by Datamonitor in the year 2000 looked at how these people had become millionaires. Although a percentage did inherit or win their fortune, the vast majority earned it themselves. So how's it done? How did they do it?

Maybe it's all about education...

In my naive formative years I thought I'd got it cracked. It was simple. Everyone said how crucial education was. Get a good education, go to University, get good qualifications and the money will follow. After all, if you're better qualified (brighter?) than 95 per cent of the population, you'll make more money than 95 per cent of the population - right? Well not quite.

I'd got a couple of things wrong. The first was that there's little correlation between education and earnings. Many of the positions which a first class education prepares you for are not particularly well paid.

Become a teacher, a local government executive, a librarian or a civil servant and you won't starve, but you might not make much more than a long distance lorry driver with nothing more prestigious than a HGV licence to his name.

Even what seemed to be "really well paid" jobs didn't (and still don't) offer much potential for the accumulation of wealth. A GP earns around £45,000 a year, an average head teacher around £30,000 and a provincial Barrister around £40,000. All of these are well above the average, but offer no chance of millionaire status.

Just work it out. If any of these people were to save all of their salary (what would they live on?) and pay no tax at all (that would be nice!) how long would they have to work to accumulate a million pounds? It's not going to happen is it? And just to make you doubly miserable, as I said in my introduction, a million pounds is not considered enough to make one rich these days. Comfortable, but not rich.

The other thing I didn't really understand was how education constrains people, forcing them down paths which their qualifications dictate they should take - the 'professional' path rather than the one they would otherwise choose. Heavy pressure is frequently placed on well qualified people to not 'waste' their education... "You've qualified for it, so you're going to do it!"

I once saw an interesting interview on television with Sir Jimmy Saville. He said he would be forever grateful that he left school at 14 because it removed any pressure from him. Nothing was expected of him so he was able to embark on a course of his own choosing, which he did to his great financial benefit.

Charles Dunstone, co-founder of The Carphone Warehouse expressed a similar view. Although he attended an expensive public school, he never shined academically, and took a job in sales rather than going to university. "If you leave school with few qualifications," he says, "you've got nothing to lose, and you're quite happy to go and set up a business. If you're more successful, you go and join Arthur Anderson (Management Consultants) or something. Me, I was working as a salesman. If this hadn't worked out, I could have got a very similar job and lost absolutely nothing."

Education gives you something which is very dangerous for someone who needs to do what is necessary to make a lot of money - something to lose.

I well remember coming out of college to the somewhat disconcerting sight of one of my former classmates (he was actually a long standing member of the remedial class, but it was the same school) pulling up in a brand new Jaguar. All bought and paid for legitimately with the profits from the three successful businesses he'd set up while I was still reading about it!

Many of the millionaires of the 1980s and 1990s owed little of their success to education. Richard Branson left school at 16 with a few O-levels. Alan Sugar, George Walker and many like them graduated from what is often called 'The University of Life.' This kind of background offers several advantages to the aspiring rich.

Firstly, there's this lack of expectation and constraint I've talked about. Secondly, with the lack of constraint comes a lack of guilt. Many well educated people feel duty bound to use their education for the common good - to put something back. Virtuous as this may be, putting something back before you've got enough out is not the route to great riches. Sorry to be so blunt, but if you want to work for the common good, don't complain if you don't get rich.

The third big advantage is a common touch, which higher education can often dull or erase altogether. If you're going to get rich, you're going to have to either earn a lot of money from a few people (very difficult), or more likely, a little money from a lot of people. So you're going to have to provide something which 'ordinary' people want.

Someone once said that nobody ever went broke underestimating the tastes of the public. The corollary of that is this: Lots of people have got very rich by offering products and services which the well educated would sneer or laugh at.

Education, and the middle class values which go with it, can blunt the appetite for trading in some of the products and services which make people rich. Education often leads people to take on middle class values irrespective of their background, which in turn have been copied from the upper classes who have historically looked down on 'trade' (Paradoxically, the upper classes have been quicker to shift from this view than the middle classes, as anyone who's recently visited a stately home gift shop will testify). 'The University of Life' entrepreneur has no such hang-ups however.

So what am I saying... that education is totally counter-productive in the quest for great wealth? Not at all. The information gathering and analysis skills acquired in higher education, combined with entrepreneurial effort, resilience and pragmatism, can create an almost unstoppable money making force.

But education on its own won't do it for you, and some of the values and views picked up in the higher education system might actually hold you back.

Okay, so maybe start-up capital is the key...

In the serial excuse maker's *Book of Extremely Useful Excuses - Volume I,* a lack of capital is an excellent standby, should the lack of education option fail to hold water. I've lost count of the number of people who've told me they would have been rich by now - if only they'd had the money to get their fantastic idea/invention/business/ project off the ground. These people are kidding themselves.

I once saw a manager from Barclays Bank being interviewed on TV. His job was to advise Pools winners who'd come into large sums of money. He said that many winners told him that now they had the money, they would like to start the business they'd always dreamed of. The bank manager invariably advised against it.

He said that true entrepreneurs don't wait to come into money before launching a business. They either start a business that doesn't require capital, find a wealthy backer, or borrow the money. The fact that these pools winners had done none of these things told him everything he needed to know about their chances of making a go of the business.

When I launched my first business, I chose one that didn't need any start up capital. My total investment in my current companies which turn over in excess of £5 million a year was £500. That's right, only £500. And I wasted most of that on stuff that I didn't really need.

Later in the book, we're going to be looking at a number of businesses requiring little or no start-up capital. So we can lay this excuse to rest once and for all.

Perhaps 'youth' is the answer then...

Sorry, but I'm not letting you off with the 'I'm too old' argument either. No matter how old you are now, I guarantee I can find someone ten years older saying that they could really start to make some money...if only they were ten years younger.

Very recently I was speaking to a man who expressed this 'too old' view. He had a great idea for a very lucrative money making project, but felt he had left it too late. His reasoning was that he intended to retire from work in five years time. I resisted the temptation to tell him that by pursuing his dream, he would be able to stop working straight away.

If you're at all tempted by the 'too old' argument, I'd suggest you ask yourself a simple question - what exactly have you got planned for the rest of your days? Is it more exciting, fulfilling and rewarding than stopping working and making a million pounds instead?

Do It Now!

You may or may not recognise the name Lenny McLean. In the 1970s and early 1980s he was 'king' of the unlicensed boxing ring. When he wasn't fighting men in the ring he was fighting them outside it as a bare knuckle fighter, minder, debt collector and doorman - the sort of character for whom the word 'colourful' was invented!

In later years McLean moved into TV and films in small supporting roles, and his last appearance was in the hit film *Lock, Stock and Two Smoking Barrels*. I say last appearance, because while making the film he was diagnosed with terminal cancer and died soon after.

Now, up until being issued with a 'death sentence,' Lenny McLean had always relied on his physical attributes and presence to make a living. He realised that this avenue was no longer open to him, and not only that, but decades of hitting and being hit had done little to benefit him financially. In short, he was effectively broke, and he knew that when he died his wife would have nothing.

It's said that necessity is often the mother of invention, and it dawned on McLean that the value in what he'd been doing for the last 30 odd years was not in the work he'd done, but in the story he could tell. And so he decided to write his autobiography. It was entitled *The Guv'nor* - McLean's ring nickname.

When the book was published, it was an immediate hit and remained firmly placed in the Top Ten Best Sellers list for at least two years. I wouldn't be at all surprised if the autobiography ultimately earns far more than Lenny McLean made from his other activities throughout his entire career.

Sadly, he isn't around to benefit - and that's the point. This book could have been written at any time and Lenny Mclean would have been able to enjoy the benefits, but it took something catastrophic to shift him out of his comfort zone and into a new, better and more lucrative course of action. In reality, most of us are like this. We have ambitions, we think there's probably a better way, we suspect there's more out there for us, but our current life isn't so bad. And so inertia gets in the way and stops us from taking the actions necessary to move on.

Yes, we want more money, yes we want an independent income, yes we want to do something more interesting than a mundane job every day, but before that can happen we have to do something. We have to take action. And that's the difficult bit.

That's why we wait - to be made redundant... for an ailing business to finally collapse... for a milestone birthday... for New Year's Day... to become ill or disabled... whatever, before finally doing something positive. If we're fortunate and it's not too late, everything works out well, our new path is successful and we go from strength to strength.

Great! But why did we wait to be forced into a corner, or for some false and meaningless future date, before doing it? After all, we can never get that wasted time back - the time between being able to do it and actually doing so. I think Mark Twain summed it up perfectly when he said:

"Twenty years from now, you'll be more disappointed by the things you didn't do than the ones you did do. So throw off the bow lines. Sail away from the safe harbour. Catch the trade winds in your sails. Explore, dream, discover."

It's a great quote, and so true. Speak to most people in the later years of their lives and you will rarely hear talk of things that they wish they hadn't done; but plenty of talk about opportunities which have now passed, and which should have been seized upon at the time.

Three of the saddest words to start any sentence are "If only I'd..." How many times have you heard them? Or more to the point - how many times have you used them yourself?

Can you imagine anyone lying on their death bed, with a saddened look in their eyes, and saying "I wish I'd spent a bit more time in that dead end job"? Neither can I. But the truth is that millions lie there wishing that they'd chased their dream; that they'd taken that chance...

So Give It A Shot!

I'm not suggesting that you be reckless and burn all your boats. However, I am suggesting that you at least push them out of the ultra safe harbour they're in right now, and see where they might take you. If it's not a place to your liking, you can always come back - feeling wiser and better for the experience.

In this chapter, what I've tried to do is make sure that you're comfortable with the fact that it's okay to want to be rich, that it's well within your grasp to achieve it, and if it's nagging away at you... essential that you try - now! I hope I've succeeded, because if not, you're not going to be able to make the best of what follows.

CHAPTER 3

The Six Golden Rules

DO YOU LIKE rules? Neither do I. It sounds too much like something you had to stick to at school. I toyed with the idea of calling this section something else - six golden suggestions, maybe - but on reflection, that sounds a bit weak and lilly-livered.

And then I thought, "to hell with it." These six things are so important, so central to you having any chance of stopping working and making a million pounds instead, that rules are what they are!

I can't over-emphasise this enough... if you're to reach the goal expressed in the title of this book, you'll need to accept and embrace each of these golden rules.

Rule No.1: Believe it!

During the 1998 football World Cup, a lot of media attention was focused on Michael Owen, the then 18 year-old Liverpool player who had made such an impact on the game. In one TV news item it emerged that Owen went to the same school as a number of other professional footballers, including Ian Rush and Gary Speed.

Owen is a far from isolated case. Jack Charlton explained in his autobiography how it was a common practice for boys from his village to go away to play professional football. He was one of a long line, which continued afterwards with his brother Bobby, and many others.

This phenomenon is not confined to football, or even the world of sport. Interviews with pop stars and other professional entertainers frequently reveal that they went to the same school as, or were brought up a few streets from, some other famous person who preceded them.

So does this kind of thing happen purely by chance? Is it something in the gene pool of a particular area which makes the inhabitants better at one thing or another? Or maybe it's something they put in the water. It has nothing to do with any of these things.

Let's say you're a working class lad who likes music and you teach yourself to play guitar. You want to be in a band... you want to be rich and famous... so you practice and start to get good - probably as good as anyone making a living from it. However, none of your family or friends are interested in music and you don't know anyone who makes a living from music, let alone anyone who's made it big.

You don't have a role model, you don't have an example to follow, so you begin to doubt that you can make it. Why should you make it? No one from your school or area ever has, so why should you? Eventually this negative feeling becomes self-fulfilling as you practice less, stop pushing quite as hard, and settle into a mediocre existence.

Now let's again imagine you are a working class lad from Manchester... same ability, same interest, but this time you live just round the corner from where the Gallagher brothers (from the massively successful group Oasis, if you didn't already know) were brought up. You go to the same school as they did. You share their background. Everybody tells you how 'normal' they were... just like everyone else in the area.

Do you think you'd believe you could make it too? Could you think of a single reason why you shouldn't follow in their footsteps? Do you think this would cause you to practice harder, commit yourself more, push harder... in fact all the things which are necessary for success? Of course it would!

In order to achieve anything, whether in sport, entertainment, a career or business, it is essential that you first believe that it can be done. If you don't believe that something can be done, then it can't...at least not by you. Your belief will impact on your actions, which in turn will ensure you get the results you expect, good bad or indifferent.

You can't create a role model for yourself, and I can't create one for you. If you don't know anyone personally who has achieved what you want to achieve then there's nothing you can do about it, but it doesn't matter. Once you understand the power of belief, and the central role it plays in success or failure, you can short circuit the system.

If you accept that you can multiply your chances of success simply by believing that at can be done, then that is enough to set a self-fulfilling prophecy in action which makes the result you're looking for all the more likely.

You might not have a history in your family, area, social circle or whatever, of people reaching the goal you've set yourself, but that shouldn't matter. Just keep in mind that, although you don't know them personally, there are people just like you who have done it. Remember that there are over 100,000 millionaires in the UK. Believe you can follow them, and the chances are multiplied that you will. I'm going to explore this in a bit more depth when we get into the related concepts of perception and expectation a little later.

Rule No.2: Invest In Yourself

Do you really want to make a huge pile of cash? It seems a stupid question doesn't it? Of course you want it. We all do, don't we? Why else would you be reading this?

Okay, let me put it another way. How much are you prepared to do to make it happen? How far are you prepared to go and what are you prepared to give up to make it a reality? A bit more tricky that one, isn't it?

The popularity of the National Lottery shows beyond any doubt that a large proportion of the population want to be rich... seriously rich. And most of us equate that, at least in part, with success. But we're not prepared to do anything more towards making it happen than putting a line through six numbers on a red ticket once a week.

Why? Because people are greedy, but they are also lazy... an unhealthy combination guaranteed to leave 99.9 per cent of those affected both disappointed and unfulfilled. They want the rewards, but without the effort. Don't believe it? Consider this - if people weren't greedy, they wouldn't enter the lottery in the first place. If they weren't lazy as well, there'd be just as many people desperately trying to earn their fortune as there are trying to win it. There aren't!

Believe it or not, I have had people send me their lottery tickets as some kind of perverse proof that they can't possibly afford the materials which might set them on the road to a money making enterprise. They have a £10 a week lottery commitment which must come first. Sad, but true!

One of my company's newsletters, *Streetwise Confidential*, details both conventional and unconventional ways of making and saving money. Do you know which section of the newsletter we get the most letters about? The excellent business opportunities? The sound money saving information? The innovative American ideas and products ready for import? The personal development ideas? No! It's the gambling systems... potential big money for no effort and no sacrifices. The greedy and lazy person's favourite section.

And that's from people who are sufficiently switched on to seek out success-building information. Just imagine what the rest of the population are like.

Now don't misunderstand me. The gambling information is both fascinating and effective, and many subscribers turn a steady regular profit from it. But it's not the most important. It should be peripheral to a money making strategy rather than central to it. The fact that more letters come in about gambling systems than anything else is disappointing, but bears out what I'm saying.

The bottom line is that although everyone claims to want success and money, only a very select few are prepared to make even minor sacrifices to bring it about. The rest trot out the same tried and tested excuses they always have:

"I don't have the time."

Solution: Try cutting out Coronation Street and Eastenders for a start. Stay out of the pub.

"I don't have any money at all."

Solution: Start by giving up drinking and smoking, cut out the luxuries (and the lottery tickets), get together in partnership with someone who's got money, or borrow some.

"I don't have the skills."

Solution: Take a course, teach yourself, or go into partnership with someone who has.

"I'm too old/young/fat/thin/tall/short" (or 'too' anything else you can think of)

Solution: Stop talking complete rubbish!

Of course, people offer all kinds of excuses, but never the underlying reason holding them back: *"Well the truth is, I'm just too damned lazy to do anything more than talk about doing something positive, and fill out my lottery ticket of course."*

There are legitimate reasons for not being able to take the actions necessary to ensure success, but 99 out of 100 people don't have one!

So do you really want success? You do? The good news is that most people are so lazy, so unwilling to make even the smallest sacrifice and the tiniest effort, that anyone who does is already head and shoulders above the mediocre crowd. To succeed, you don't need to work ten hours a day and you don't need to give up everything you enjoy, but you do need to be a little less lazy and a little more willing to make sacrifices than average.

Not prepared to do it? Well stop reading, put your feet up, fill out your lottery ticket and dream on. Don't feel bad about it... you're far from alone. Still with me? Good...

So are you ready to invest in yourself? I don't know about you, but when I hear the word "investment" my eyes start to glaze over. It's probably because the word is usually used in the context of financial matters. With all due respect to any financial advisors or bank managers reading this, investment just isn't very interesting is it?

But it's not merely about bank accounts, stocks and shares and pension funds. The purpose of any investment is to secure a return, to get something back in excess of what was invested in the first place. The higher the return, the better the investment. Here's the key though - in order to get something out, you first have to put something in. You don't get any return unless you put in first. So it's a case of one step back to take two steps forward.

And it's exactly the same situation when you're making the most important investment of all... an investment in yourself. Sadly, a lot of people seem reluctant to make any investment in themselves, either in time or money. Let me give you an example:

One of my company's most successful and popular products is a home study course in Private Investigation. Since 1994, hundreds of people have used the course as a springboard to a lucrative new full or part-time career in this growing field. The course costs around £150, and a professional investigator can expect to earn around £18 an hour for his or her expertise. I'm sure you'll agree that this is an excellent potential return on a course which costs the equivalent of eight hours earnings.

Yet every week we receive a handful of letters from people who claim that private investigation is what they've always wanted to do, but they can't take the course because either:

1. They can't raise the £150 course fees, or
2. They don't have time to study.

If you stop to think about this for a moment, it's hard to know whether to laugh or cry. Here is someone who has found something they really want to do, but is not prepared to invest a small amount of money, or a few hours each week, to achieve their goal. You might initially be tempted to feel sorry for these people for their poverty or busy schedule. But in almost every case your sympathy would be misplaced!

The people claiming they can't raise £150 to learn how to do something they've always wanted - and earn £18 an hour in the process - invariably own the latest home entertainment products and drive a car (secured on finance) just that little bit more expensive than they can afford.

But so what? It impresses the neighbours.

It doesn't stop them going for a night out either: "You've got to enjoy yourself haven't you? In the long run, you're dead." Speaking of which, it doesn't stop them puffing their way through packs of health wrecking cigarettes, if the smoky stench rising from some of the letters I open is any indication.

The sad fact is that most people would rather spend money on items which are either consumed (alcohol, meals out, cigarettes) or can never provide any return (cars, TVs, Hi-Fis etc.) than make an investment in themselves which will ultimately pay back many times over.

The irony is, of course, that an investment in yourself will normally lead to a return which comfortably allows you to purchase all the 'toys' you are currently struggling to afford.

Time is the other investment which people are often reluctant to make. Too busy to study/learn/ research? Maybe, but apparently not too busy to spend hours in the pub or slumped in front of the TV watching some overexcited cretin trying to decide whether the next card will be higher or lower than the previous one. Is that really more important than working towards future success?

The key word there, of course, is 'future.' An investment in yourself, of either time or money, will not give an instant return. You're going to have to wait for the benefit, while you could opt to have your new car, TV, pint of Guinness or packet of Benson & Hedges today if you wanted to.

Deferred Gratification

Given the choice of £1,000 today or £3,000 in two years time, the great majority of people would take the £1,000 today. Don't believe it? Ask around and you'll see. When you do, you'll see something else: that the people who opt for the £3,000 in two years are the most successful ones.

And that's not because they don't need the ready cash. It's because they understand the need for deferred gratification... giving something up now in return for something far better in the future. And that's what investing in yourself is all about.

Deferred gratification and the related concepts of investing in yourself and in your future are essential building blocks in any success or money making strategy. No one ever achieved anything of note (except by good fortune) without accepting and embracing this basic truth.

If you're still in any doubt about the importance of investing in yourself, consider the following idea, for which I'm indebted to Peter Thomson, one of the country's top personal development writers and speakers:

Imagine for a moment that you run a business, and you are allowed just one employee. Not only that, but it's the only employee you're ever going to have. You can't sack him, you can't employ an assistant. Nothing! It's just you and him for ever.

So let me ask you this. How are you going to treat that employee? Are you going to train him, nurture him, invest time and money in him? Of course you are. It would be foolish to do anything else.

Well in the business of 'You Limited,' you're the only employee you're ever going to have. You're stuck with yourself for life. So doesn't it make sense to invest in and develop that employee in whatever ways are necessary to make the enterprise a success?

Give some serious thought to this, and in what areas the investment is needed most.

Rule No.3: Take Responsibility

A few years ago, at what seemed to be at the time, the height of the property boom, a couple purchased a house in London with the express intention of making some improvements and turning round a quick profit. Nothing wrong with that. But in order to buy the house, they needed a massive loan - somewhere in excess of £300,000. They took the idea to their bank manager who happily gave them the money.

To cut a long story short, the housing market collapsed before they could renovate and sell the property. The couple made a substantial loss, and so they sued their bank for giving negligent advice in letting them have the money in the first place. The case went to court, and the couple won damages of some £70,000 against Lloyds Bank.

How do you react to that story? Do you share the general euphoria which greeted the decision in the media? The little guy getting one over on big business - or do you share my view? Your answer could tell you a lot about how well suited you are to an independent, entrepreneurial lifestyle... the sort of lifestyle which will allow you to stop working and make a million pounds instead.

Let me make one thing clear. I'm no great defender of banks. They charge too much money for too little service, and for the most part, are only prepared to help when you don't need them. But there is a more important principle at stake here. In a word, responsibility.

The couple in this case entered into a money making venture. If it had succeeded they would have made many thousands of pounds for very little effort. Great! But it didn't succeed. Through circumstances which neither they nor their bank foresaw, the market changed and they were left high and dry.

So why should the bank take the responsibility? It was not their project, and they did not stand to make the easy profits if it succeeded, so why should they make the loss when it failed? This case highlighted both the shift away from accepting individual responsibility in society in general, and one of the major reasons for the failure of money making ventures in particular.

To succeed in any effort, it is essential that you accept full responsibility for the outcome. Starting out with any other attitude almost guarantees failure. It's true in business and it's true in life. Teenagers who are told that their criminal behaviour is a result of social deprivation will carry on, secure in the knowledge that it's someone else's fault. Business people who believe that the economy is dying on its feet will sit back, secure in the knowledge that their failure can be laid at the governments door. It's all depressingly self fulfilling.

Don't deceive yourself. Whatever ventures you undertake - accept responsibility. *The outcome is down to you... no excuses.*

Just as soon as you do that, a miraculous thing will happen - your chances of success will multiply. It's easy to blame someone else, but not so easy to blame yourself. When there's someone else to blame, it's so tempting to give up at the first hurdle ("the bank wouldn't give me any money," "the customers didn't see what a good product I had," "my suppliers let me down," "there's too much competition").

When you accept full responsibility for the outcome yourself, you won't give up ("let's try another bank... and another," "let's see how else we can sell it," "let's find another source of supply," or "how can we provide a better service than the competition").

I read recently that Colonel Sanders, at the age of 66, approached over 2,000 restaurants with his idea for Kentucky Fried Chicken before he found one which would give it a chance. How many would you have approached? Five? Ten?

Most of us would have given up long before, not blaming ourselves of course, but rather the damn fool restaurant owners who wouldn't know a good idea it it jumped up and bit them. Sanders took full responsibility. He had no intention of blaming anyone else, and as a result, he had no reason to.

Just the other day, I read that J K Rowling was turned down by 12 publishers before she found one who would publish her *Harry Potter* books. It would have been so easy for her to bemoan the fact that the publishers just wouldn't give a chance to a single mum writing adventure stories primarily for boys, and give up. She didn't and now she's at least £50 million richer - and with a great deal more to come.

I can guide you towards the very best money making ideas (and I will later in the book) but they will be of little value unless you are prepared to do one thing. Do yourself the most massive favour you can. Take full responsibility for the outcome of every project you undertake from day one. Your successes will be all the sweeter and your failures all the rarer.

Rule No.4: Play The Hand You've Been Dealt

Every year the World Series of Poker is held in Las Vegas - the world championship of the game. It's a game with, seemingly, a large element of chance attached. The players can, after all, only play with the cards they're dealt.

In the long term, the law of averages dictates that luck will be pretty evenly distributed amongst the players. You would therefore expect that the outcome of matches will fluctuate widely depending on the varying fortunes of those taking part. That's not what happens. Although results do vary, the same players perform consistently well, irrespective of the cards they're dealt. And it's the same in life.

It's all too easy to complain about the cards you've been dealt and use that as an excuse for failure. The top 'players' accept the cards they're given - there's nothing you can do about that - and then work out how best to use them to get the results they're after. Even when people are dealt great cards, it's all too easy to waste them.

At the risk of boring anyone not interested in football, it does provide us with an excellent example, showing why the 'cards' you're dealt is less important than how they are used.

There can be few footballers dealt a better 'hand' than George Best. Most experts agree that he was one of the most naturally gifted players of all time, and yet by the age of 26, when he should have been at his best, he virtually disappeared from the game, as did his opportunity to become the richest and most successful player of his generation. Few have achieved so little with so much.

At the same time as Best was ending his career, Kevin Keegan was just starting his. He was too small, too thin, and by his own admission, lacked great natural footballing ability. It would have been all too easy for him to give in to the hand he'd been dealt, and accept that he would never be a top player because he didn't have Best's ability. But through hard work and determination he rose to become captain of his country and to win practically every honour in the game, making himself a not inconsiderable fortune in the process.

Hard work and determination are not the only ways to overcome a terrible 'hand.' So for the moment, I'm going to stick with my football analogy...

A player who few would place in the 'gifted' category is Vinny Jones. In fact, few would place him in their pub first team if footballing skill were the sole criteria! And yet he consistently played in the top division, represented his country, and made a lot of money in the process. There are literally thousands of 'Vinny Joneses' out there, but few get to play professionally at all. Certainly hard work and determination played a part, but so did a commitment to playing the game on his own terms.

If Vinny Jones had tried to play the game like George Best, he wouldn't have lasted five minutes. What he had to do was establish his strengths and play to them. He concentrated on what he could do, not what he couldn't. Occasionally that may have meant bending some of the rules, but that's what 'ordinary' players have to do sometimes to stay in the game.

Jones was to prove that what he achieved in football was no fluke. He later used the same flare for playing his 'hand' to the maximum in a completely separate field - and one which he would seem equally ill-suited. Vinny Jones the footballer became Vinny Jones the Hollywood film star. Just as he didn't try to emulate Best on the football field, he didn't try to emulate Gielgud, Olivier or even Robert Redford on screen. But he did play the hand he had been dealt to great effect.

While we're on the subject of Hollywood film stars, Arnold Schwarzenegger and Danny De Vito are examples of two more people dealt a seemingly impossible hand, but having the intelligence and determination to turn it into a winning one.

It doesn't take a massive leap of logic to see that there's a message here for anyone aiming for a business or personal goal. You may not have been dealt the hand of a Pele or a George Best, but that should not be taken as a barrier to success.

The key to success is accepting your hand (you won't get another one!) and adapting to it where necessary. Certainly it may involve hard work, and you may have to make the rules work for you, rather than the other way round. But the end result when you achieve it will be all the more rewarding.

Rule No.5: Choose your advisors carefully

Every day, I receive letters and phone calls from people keen - desperate even - to gain some financial independence and start making some money in a venture or series of ventures. What's more, I hear from them at various stages of their business development. I see people succeed, and I see why they succeed. I also see people fail, and see the reasons for that as well. I've touched on some of those already.

Probably the most depressing of all are the people who don't get started at all. They have no hope of success. From the letters and phone calls I get, there are all sorts of reasons why people simply don't get started in a venture which originally excited and inspired them. Some (but not many) are valid. But there is one which stands head and shoulders above the rest. It is responsible for more abandoned take-offs than all the rest put together. What is it? Other people's advice.

I've received numerous letters and phone calls which go something along the lines of: "I think it's a great idea, but I had a word with my wife/brother/father/mate Fred, and he/she doesn't think it will work, so I'm not going to do it." Amazing isn't it? Believe me, it happens all the time.

It's natural to discuss ideas, ambitions and plans with people you're close to. We all do it. But taking advice and guidance is something different. It's one thing to take advice from someone who has already trod the same or similar path. It's quite another to alter your plans on the basis of 'off the cuff' comments from someone who has little or no knowledge, and whose opinion is based on nothing of any substance.

They will often have heard of someone who tried 'something similar,' but it didn't work. Not only that, but they ended up bankrupt, in the work house and eventually committed suicide in a fit of depression! So be warned.

Haven't you read about and researched the idea? Don't you know a great deal more about it than the person you're discussing it with? Then why on earth would you put their opinion above your own? Politely listen, but be sure to separate out hard facts from hearsay, vagaries and plain twaddle. All this assumes of course, that the advice you get from those around you is well meaning, if inaccurate. It's not necessarily the case. Everyone has their own hidden agenda, and it almost certainly won't be the same as yours.

Fred may well be your best mate, but it doesn't stop him being jealous of the fact that you've got a great idea which is probably going to make you much better off than him. He failed in an attempt to set up in business a few years ago and now it looks as though you're going to succeed. What better way to stop that happening than to pour cold water on your idea? Your wife or husband may love you but it doesn't mean that they want to spend more time alone while you set up your new enterprise in your spare time, does it? What better way to stop that happening than to run down the idea?

Do you understand the point I'm making? Other people will have all sorts of reasons for discouraging you, which have little or nothing to do with the viability of the venture itself. To give up through this kind of discouragement is a crying shame and a waste.

One of the things that business books always tell you is to take professional advice before entering into a business. By professional advice they mean bankers, solicitors and accountants. When purchasing a business as a going concern there is some logic to this. You may need to borrow money from the bank, get the solicitor to look at the contract of sale, and have the accountant make sure that the books are in order.

But entrepreneurial start-ups are a little different. I've often spoken to a client who is incredibly excited about an opportunity, but says: "I just want to get the opinion of my bank manager/accountant/solicitor first."

Bear in mind that these are opportunities which involve no start up cost, no borrowing, no legal entanglements, and there are no books to examine.

Why would you seek out the opinion of these people? You may just as well consult your hairdresser or garage mechanic. In fact that would probably be a better option since those people may actually have experience of setting up and running a small enterprise. Your professional advisors will almost certainly not have that experience.

So who should you consult? One piece of advice given to budding entrepreneurs is to associate with, learn from and emulate successful people - those who have already made their mark. This is sound advice, but there's a problem. How do you know who these people are?

On the face of it, it seems simple. Look at where they live, the car they drive, the lifestyle they appear to lead, and you'll find the achievers who can help lead you down the path to success. If only it were that simple! I was reminded of this when on a recent trip to the United States, I came across a book entitled *The Millionaire Next Door* (Longstreet Press) by Tom Stanley and Bill Danko. It makes fascinating reading. The authors have studied millionaires since 1973 and find that they are far from the easily identifiable conspicuous consumers most of us have been led to believe. Most of the successful people in Stanley and Danko's study avoided showing off their wealth altogether:

- They were more likely to drive a secondhand Ford than a new Jaguar or Rolls Royce.
- They shunned designer clothing in favour of 'off the peg' chain store items, and expensive jewellery was not high on their list of priorities.
- Most lived in fairly modest houses and ate out at mid-range restaurants.

One thing they all had in common was that they lived well below their means. Only their bank accounts would give a clue to their true wealth, and nobody saw those.

If that's the situation in the United States, where the prevailing attitude to wealth and success is to admire it and aspire to it, how do you think the truly successful in this country behave, where the attitude is much more negative? You don't have to think too hard to realise that what you see is not necessarily what you get. In fact, it sometimes seems that everyone is trying to create an impression completely at odds with the truth.

Most people who come to my office with some proposal or other, arrive in an impressive car - a Mercedes, Porsche, BMW or the like, wearing expensive designer clothes - the very picture of affluence and success. Yet almost without exception, something very interesting emerges as our meeting progresses. They don't have any money!

I don't mean they're not rich. I mean they're worse than flat broke - their car is on finance, they're mortgaged up to the hilt and they can't even find a few hundred pounds to get their idea off the ground. And yet to the outside world they're wealthy and successful, people to be emulated. They must be - just look at what they've got!

Some of the worst 'offenders' of this type are those involved in MLM or Network Marketing, and with good reason. Their whole business is based on persuading people that their success is something to be aspired to and copied. I well remember attending an MLM recruitment meeting several years ago. I've never seen so many flashy cars in the car park, or Rolex watches on wrists. But, as I was to quickly find out, the cars were on full finance, the watches were fake, and most of people trying to persuade everyone else to follow them had yet to make a penny themselves!

Before I get a flood of letters from irate networkers, let me emphasise that there are genuine participants making good money. But even the most ardent networker would accept that this way of doing business attracts more than its fair share of false prophets.

On the other side of the coin, rarely a month goes by without a newspaper article being published about some apparently penniless old man leaving a fortune in his will. Nobody knew of his vast wealth or how he acquired it. It is these low profile success stories that are the most fascinating and potentially revealing, not the half truths put forward by the fast car, fast talk merchants.

By all means mix with, learn from and emulate successful people, but first make sure that they're the genuine article. To do so, you're probably going to have to dig below the surface. They could just as easily be driving a Renault as a Roller, just as likely to be living in a maisonette as a mansion. Face value is no value.

So choose your advisors carefully. Discuss your ideas and plans with others, but don't allow yourself to be sidetracked or stopped by those who are either ignorant of the subject altogether, or have their own agendas.

Rule No.6: Persist...Persist...Persist...

I once watched a superb wildlife programme about the African honey badger. Now don't be under any misapprehension here. This animal is nothing like the cuddly, shy creatures we know and love. Imagine a pitbull in a badger suit and you'll get the idea.

Anyway, as the name suggests, this animal is particularly fond of honey. With the African bush being notably short of Sainsburys branches the only source of food available to the badger is bee hives - with lots of bees in them.

Watching the honey badger go about its work was fascinating. Having located a hive in a hollowed out tree it cleared out debris to make a wider entrance. The reason would soon become clear: it was going to need an escape route, and it knew it.

The badgers first foray into the hive was painful to watch. It was attacked systematically by the bees and got only a small mouthful of honey before withdrawing to lick its wounds. At this point you expected the badger to give up having learned a painful lesson. Not a bit of it!

Time after time it went back into the hive, getting stung each time and only getting small amounts of honey in return. You almost found yourself screaming "For God's sake, don't go back in!," as another visit resulted in more pain.

But as time went on, a funny thing happened. The stings got less and less as the stinging bees died off, and the badger came away with more and more booty on each visit. Eventually, the bees gave up the fight and the badger made off into the bush with the entire hive. Victory, from what appeared initially to be a hopeless quest.

The badger knew the job wasn't going to be easy from the start. He knew he wasn't going to get something for nothing, and that pain would inevitably precede pleasure. By clearing out the entrance to the hive he was preparing for the numerous tactical withdrawals which he knew would be necessary. But what he also knew was that if he kept at the job, if he persisted, eventually the resistance would be broken down and his goal would be reached.

Of course, he had an alternative. After going into the hive for the first time and getting stung so badly for so little he could have thought: "This isn't worth it. I'll go and find an easier hive." But he didn't, because he knew that all hives are difficult, and if you want the honey you just have to buckle down and do what's necessary.

I'm sure the lesson of this isn't lost on you. So many would-be entrepreneurs give up when entering 'the hive' for the first time, after receiving the inevitable 'stings' and getting very little in return. They decide to go and look for another 'hive' where the bees aren't as fierce.

When that 'hive' proves equally difficult, they give up again and go to the next, and the next, and the next... Entering every 'hive' involves getting stung, and so our entrepreneur gets stung again and again, and with very little reward because each time they're starting on a new 'hive' where the defences are at their most intense.

For 'hive' - read business or venture; for 'sting' - read problems, difficulties, or obstacles, and you'll get the picture. No matter what business or venture you start there will be difficulties, and they will be at their most intense in the early stages. Giving up to look for something easier when these difficulties present themselves will prove to be a fruitless exercise. The next venture will carry with it a whole new set of difficulties for you to deal with.

I once knew a young man whose 'success' with the opposite sex was legendary. I'm not talking about the kind of success that results in the development of long term relationships! It was a little more basic than that, if you get my meaning. Anyway, to anyone who knew him, it was difficult to understand. He was under height, overweight and hardly the most appealing sight you've ever seen. In short, Tom Cruise had nothing to worry about.

Purely in the interests of research, I once asked him what his secret was. "It's easy," he said. "I just walk up to every girl I like the look of and say: 'Would you like to...?'"
To protect those of a delicate disposition, I won't repeat the full question here (there's only one more word to it, by the way), suffice to say it was not particularly subtle or polite.

Somewhat horrified, I asked him whether this didn't result in some robust and irate responses. "Of course," he replied. "Some of them slap me across the face and others just tell me to f*** off, but if you ask enough, someone always eventually says 'yes.'"

A few years ago I worked with a salesman. He had an almost god given knack of alienating, upsetting and offending everyone he met. He had any number of ways of achieving this. You would almost think it was deliberate, but I don't think it was. This man's sales figures were actually the best in the company, by quite some margin - not what you'd expect from someone who was guaranteed to disenchant every new prospect within seconds of meeting them.

Intrigued by the anomaly, I was pleased to have the opportunity to accompany the man on some of his sales calls. At first I thought that he must deal with his customers differently to everyone else. Not so! He was equally obnoxious. So how did he succeed? Simple really. He asked everyone whether they wanted to buy, even when it was patently obvious to anyone with an ounce of sensitivity that they did not.

When they told him they weren't interested, he ignored them! When they told him politely to leave them alone, he pretended not to notice. Or maybe he didn't notice. Then he asked them again, and kept asking until they said "yes." I'm convinced that some people ordered just to get rid of him, but order they did. When it comes down to it, all that he had in his favour was a skin like a rhinoceros, and the tenacity to ask as many people as possible whether they would like to buy his product.

In a way, our two 'heroes' used identical techniques. Neither had any natural advantages for what they were trying to achieve. In fact, the competition were better suited to the job. And yet it was they who achieved the goal - by asking and asking and asking again, and refusing to be dispirited or deflected by temporary failure or rejection.

As I've tried to emphasise thus far, the difference between success and failure in any enterprise has little to do with how much money you have, what qualifications you have, who you know or anything like that. But it has everything to do with attitude... and following on from that, persistence.

In my experience, 99 per cent of people who embark on a business project and fail, do so for just two reasons. They either don't get started at all, or give up at the first hurdle... real or perceived. Just this week, I received a letter from a gentleman who had started an advertising based business. But it 'hadn't worked.' He'd given up.

Apparently, of the 50 businesses he'd written to about his new venture (which they knew nothing about previously) only six had expressed an intention to purchase. So 12 per cent of the mailshot had responded positively to his very first marketing effort and he took this as a signal to give up! We should all be so lucky as to get such a response from our marketing efforts.

Not all situations are as clear cut as this though. In the early days of any venture, there will inevitably be real setbacks, obstacles and problems to overcome. Very few people make their million over night. There may be times when you question whether the venture will take off at all. Every successful person goes through this stage. It's only the people who fail that don't.

I read somewhere, I think it was in a book by either Dale Carnegie or Napoleon Hill, that the majority of people give up on a venture, just at the brink of success. Unfortunately, in my experience the vast majority of people don't even allow themselves to get to the brink of success. They expect instant success and when it doesn't happen, they take the easy way out.

I was reminded of this when talking to a business contact recently. A few years ago, he'd given up a well paid job to go it alone. He made no money at all for six months and then only £2,500 in the next 12 months. Most people would have given up before this, and he certainly considered it. But he didn't. He kept going. In the 19th month, he started to turn the corner, and made £50,000 over the next year. This year, he tells me he'll make over half a million pounds. Just imagine if he'd given up after 18 months!

The bottom line is this. Unless you're very lucky, money making success will not happen straight away. It takes time. I can point you in the right direction, but I can't remove every obstacle from your path. Choose your direction, set your course and commit to seeing it through to the end.

Not one successful person has ever had a 'clear run.' You're unlikely to be the first. James Dyson, inventor of the Dyson vacuum cleaner, and now owner of a business worth several hundred million pounds put it this way, "Success is made of 99 per cent failure. You galvanise yourself and you keep going." Persistence is what saw him through in the end - just like the honey badger - and it will do the same for you.

In Summary

As you read through my six golden rules, I know you were tempted to dismiss at least some of them as obvious...things you already knew. Well I know from personal experience that there is an enormous gulf between knowing something and acting on that knowledge. Knowledge is only of any value when it's used as a basis for action.

So get these 6 foundation blocks firmly in place:

• *Believe firmly that you can do it*

• *Invest heavily in yourself*

• *Take full responsibility for all outcomes*

• *Accept the cards you've been dealt and play them to the maximum*

• *Choose Your advisors carefully*

• *Persist*

You'll multiply your chances of success in your quest to stop working and make a million pounds, many times over. In the next section, we're going to start building on these founding principles. We're going to look at the stuff you really need to know if you're going to make your million - however you intend to do it!

CHAPTER 4

Fifteen Things You Really Need To Know!

SO WE'VE GOT the foundations in place, and we're several steps nearer to the dream... stop work and make a million pounds instead - but you're not ready to take concrete action yet. There are 15 things I think you simply must know before you make any decision at all about the method you're going to use to make your pile.

These 15 things are applicable, irrespective of what money making project or projects you embark upon. It's stuff I wish I'd fully understood from day one. If I had, I reckon I'd have arrived where I am today in about half the time.

I know you're impatient - eager to start making money. Take on board the information in the next few pages and you'll get there twice as fast.

1. You Get What You Expect. So Expect More!

Welcome to my psychiatrist's chair. Make yourself comfortable, ease right back... and now I want to take you back to your childhood.

You were five years old and you saw a toy you really wanted. I mean you really wanted it badly. I don't know you personally, and I don't know how old you are (so I can't guess what the toy was), but I know there was a toy, and I know how much you wanted it. With me it was a Johnny Seven gun.

Depending on your age, it could be anything from a Hula Hoop to a Cabbage Patch Doll. In any event, you know what it was. Anyway, you went to your parents, and asked if you could have the toy for your birthday. Did they say, "Yes, of course, no problem at all." Chances are, they didn't. If they were like most parents, they said something like, "Wait and see." If you pressed them, you probably got something like "Well, if you expect, you won't get."

Whether you got the toy or not, this sort of response was something you probably became accustomed to hearing over the years... no definite commitment, and always the warning not to expect too much.

Of course, there were perfectly good reasons for this. Your parents weren't sure whether they'd be able to get the toy for you. They'd be concerned that they couldn't afford it when the time came, or that the shops would be out of stock. It was all down to them, and their response reflected that. They didn't want to disappoint you; so there was always a warning to lower your expectations, not to expect too much, because unfulfilled expectation leads to abject disappointment in your average five-year-old, and no parent wants that.

I'm sure you can see where I'm heading with this. Psychologists, personal development experts, and just about everyone else who has studied human psychology and the factors involved in success and failure, broadly agree on two important things:

1. What we learn in early childhood has a significant ongoing effect on our thinking and behaviour throughout our lives - unless we make a determined effort to re-programme and re-learn.

2. We get pretty much what we expect to get from life... and rarely more. Expectation always precedes acquisition.

So we have a situation where early childhood has created a general tendency towards low expectation. At the time it was appropriate - we had no control over the fulfillment, or otherwise, of our expectation. We'd be devastated if our expectation wasn't met.

But all that's changed now. We've grown up. We have control, and what's more, we're big enough to take it if we fall short of what we expect. Low expectations are completely at odds with achievement, monetary or otherwise. Very little of any consequence is ever achieved without the expectation and belief that it can be done - except when it happens by sheer accident.

Why? Because we only take the actions necessary to achieve success when we expect a successful outcome. In any venture, there will be setbacks and low points. The only thing that gets us through these is the belief, the expectation, that we will ultimately succeed. If we don't believe and expect that we'll ultimately triumph, why the hell should we put ourselves through the pain and difficulty of pressing on through adversity?

Can you see how high expectation must always precede high achievement, and how your early conditioning might be holding you back from achieving your full potential now? It's definitely worth taking a little time to assess whether your expectations are as high as they should be, and whether they're being created and shaped by old and obsolete influences. What you discover may surprise you.

2. It's Okay To Be Different!

The words 'eccentric' and 'millionaire' seem to be almost inextricably linked in the popular psyche. I'm not sure where it all started - maybe it was with the reclusive Howard Hughes, or the terminally tight-fisted John Paul Getty - but the tag has stuck. Anyone with a few quid in the bank and a liking for stripy trousers automatically inherits the label. And the implication is often less than flattering - that the person may be rich, but they're not quite normal.

Not really fair of course, but it does help the rest of us feel better about not being quite so wealthy! There is a serious point to all this though. You see, it seems that all millionaires - or at least those who have earned the money rather than won or inherited it - must, by definition be 'eccentric.' Here's how Webster's Dictionary defines the word:

'...deviating from an established or usual pattern or style.'

Of course millionaires deviate from an established or usual pattern or style! This is an essential pre-requisite to achieving anything worthwhile. Why? Simply because extraordinary results require extraordinary actions to bring them about.

What do you think happens if you conform to an established or usual pattern or style? That's right - you get a normal or usual result. And a normal or usual result doesn't lead to great wealth. If it did, we'd all be rich. At the moment, you may well have a negative attitude towards being non-conformist... going against the crowd. And if you do, in all likelihood, it's a hangover from your childhood.

Before we're out of nappies, we're already well down the road of indoctrination into a belief that there is a 'right way' to do everything. We are led to believe that among the many 'wrong' ways of doing something there is just one right way. Of course, when you're a kid it makes a lot of sense. The world is a new and complicated enough place as it is. The last thing you need is 12 different options for holding a spoon! And so we learn one way, and that's the right way. One way for everything.

When we start school, the same process continues. One way to write, one way to read, one way to add up, one way to sit, one way to queue for lunch, one way to hold hands with your partner on the odd outing from school. One way for everything, and one way for everyone. And so it goes on. Every school book we ever read told us the right way to do things. Rarely were we given a choice or options. This is how it's done and this is how we'll all do it, they seem to say.

Is it any wonder then, that by the time we approach adulthood this whole idea has become firmly embedded? There's a right way to do things, and it's the only acceptable way. To succeed, you have to do things that particular way. Take any other path and you'll fail. The ultimate conclusion, of course, is that there's one way to think.

This 'one right way,' middle of the road approach keeps most people safe. They are safe from harm, reasonably competent in what they do, and importantly for the rest of us, comfortable to be around. We know what they're going to do and when they're going to do it. There are no surprises, nasty or otherwise.

However, as an approach geared to maximising individual potential, it's extremely flawed. While conventional wisdom (the "one right way" approach) is usually safe, it isn't necessarily correct. Follow it in business and money making activities and the result will inevitably be mediocre. Why? Because everyone else will be doing the same thing. Follow them and you'll get the same result. Mediocre, middle of the road, average activity.

Conventional wisdom presents a picture of the successful business person dressed in a smart suit, working from prestigious offices, surrounded by eager staff. Working days are long and holidays rarely taken. Oh yes, you'll need a fancy car, mobile phone and a laptop computer! It's the 'right way' to do things.

The reality is that the people who conform to this stereotype are rarely the truly successful. They follow the middle, safe route and their achievements reflect this. Consider the truly successful, the real winners, and you'll find most to be far removed from the stereotypical 'right way' in terms of appearance and working practices. What's more, they're far removed from each other. Look at successful British entrepreneurs like James Dyson, Anita Roddick, Felix Dennis, Luke Johnson and Julian Richer and you will find a diverse and non-stereotypical group. They have their own very personal style and approach. What does this mean?

More often than not, it means that they recognised that there is 'more than one way to skin a cat,' and that an individualistic, off-beat, approach often brings about extraordinary results. It probably explains how Richard Branson can work from his home, never wear a suit or tie, and take seven weeks holiday each year. It also perhaps explains how John Paul Getty ran a multi billion dollar oil empire from his hotel room, while issuing instructions to his employees on the back of envelopes. It might even explain why Peter Stringfellow refuses to get a decent haircut! Behind these apparently superficial examples lies a basic truth. Most successful people not only behave differently to the norm, they also think outside of the norm as well. And that is what separates them from the herd.

So remember - whatever path you choose in your quest to stop working and make a million pounds instead... there is no one 'right way.'

There are any number of ways which will work. Your task is to find the one which suits you best, not the one someone else says you should take. To coin a popular phrase, dare to be different!

3. It's Okay To Fail!

Are you failing enough? Seems a strange question for a book aimed at people who want to make their million, doesn't it? And yet it's a valid one. Bear with me.

I don't know a great deal about baseball, but even I've heard of Babe Ruth. He's remembered for holding the record for the greatest number of home runs, which is a good thing... apparently! But what not many people know or remember, is that he also holds the record for the greatest number of 'strike outs,' which is a bad thing! In other words, he failed an awful lot.

Ted Nicholas is the world's best selling self published author, and as a result has accumulated a multi-million dollar fortune. And yet he will happily tell you that he is responsible for more failed advertisements than just about anyone else. As an aside, I think I've got a claim on the UK record!

Did you know that most of Richard Branson's Virgin group businesses lose money? No reason why you should, because the successful businesses more than compensate, making Branson - sorry Sir Richard - one of the richest men in the country.

I once attended a seminar hosted by Dan Pena. Dan lives in a Baronial style castle in Scotland and a beach front home in California. His fortune is vast. And yet at the seminar, he confided that during his business career, he has lost hundreds of millions of pounds, and that 40 per cent of his business decisions have been wrong.

Can you see where I'm heading with this? Here are four fabulously successful people who have had more than their fair share of failures. They're by no means unique. Look closely at any successful person, and you'll see the same thing - a great deal of failure and setback. Why is this?

It's because successful people know that in order to achieve success you must first try, and then keep trying through the adversity which will inevitably come. They also know that the greatest successes come, the closer you go to the 'edge'. And that's a place where massive success and total failure are often a hairs breadth apart.

Going for the 'big win' inevitably means that you will fall short sometimes. Aiming for an easier target means you will usually 'succeed', but the success is likely to be a minor one, and far less rewarding and satisfying as a result. On a personal note, I know that my greatest successes have been preceded by, and sometimes initiated by, a disappointment or failure which has forced me to seek out an alternative.

So are you experiencing failures? Many? If you're only achieving success and feeling quite smug about it, don't be. It just means you're not trying enough things. You're not pushing close enough to the edge. You're playing safe, and missing out on the big opportunities as a result.

Putting yourself in a position where you might fail takes courage. Many of us can't take the disappointment and blow to the ego which accompany each unsuccessful effort. And that's one of the main reasons that so few of us are destined to reach the very highest levels of success.

4. You Don't Need To Do The Thing Right - Just Do The Right Thing!

In the mid 1980s, I had a colleague whose work rate left me astonished. Whenever I saw him he was scribbling away at some paperwork or other. If I phoned him in the evening he would lose no time in telling me how I had interrupted more paperwork. Occasionally, we would meet up at conferences and sales meetings. It was the same story: paperwork scattered across his hotel room, and cursing his luck that he didn't have time to enjoy the hotel facilities.

I found all this a bit disturbing. You see, I was supposed to be doing the same job as him, and all this paperwork was something of a mystery to me. Mine took about 20 minutes once a week. I must be doing something wrong, I thought, but I couldn't work out what it was. All the same, my friend didn't seem to be making any great strides in the job, despite holding it for some 15 years. In fact, his results were worse than mine.

A few years later I was working for another company, where once a year we would get together to prepare annual budgets. It was not an exact science to say the least. The unknown factors were such that the final figures could never be anything better than a wild approximation. The whole process was supposed to take three days.

By midday on the first day I had my budget complete, only to watch with increasing levels of dismay as my colleagues took another two days to complete the same job. This was worrying. They were able people, and as someone with considerably less experience, the most sensible conclusion was that I must be at fault in some way. But the end result seemed okay, and my budget proved to be at least as accurate as anyone else's.

It took me quite some time before I figured out the important principle which underlies these apparent anomalies, which is this:

It is far more important to 'do the right thing' than it is to 'do the thing right.'

Most people are more concerned with being seen to be doing the thing right, rather than stopping to consider whether they're doing the right thing in the first place. In other words, the first decision should be to decide upon priorities and the value of tasks before undertaking them.

There is little or no point in carrying out a job to perfection which doesn't need doing, or one which isn't particularly important in the overall picture. Far better to carry out that job to an appropriate standard and allow maximum time and effort to devote to the things which really matter.

I realise this may sound obvious, but the letters I receive suggest that very few people stop to prioritise; to search out the 'right thing' to concentrate on before getting down to business.

5. And The Right Thing Is... Market First!

Like all publishers, I receive a large number of manuscripts for consideration.

As you might imagine, the quality varies. At one end of the scale I might receive a well written and researched 300 page book, and at the other nothing more than two pages of handwritten scrawl! But I welcome them all. As the saying goes... You have to kiss a lot of frogs before you find a prince.

One type of manuscript is particularly disappointing and frustrating to receive. It's not the 'two-page wonder,' written on toilet paper and littered with spelling mistakes and typographical errors. These can easily be discounted and rejected. The author has clearly put little or no work into the publication and really doesn't deserve any reward. No, the ones that disappoint most are the well written, well presented and researched manuscripts... on a subject no-one wants to read about!

I have in front of me a nicely typed, well written manuscript, submitted by a lady who has operated as an independent distributor for a number of network marketing companies over the last six years. There has to be an enlightening publication there, surely. If she'd made a lot of money in the business, then a manual detailing the precise steps she took which others could follow, would probably find a market. But she didn't make much money at all.

No matter - a book detailing the mistakes she made, and what she would do differently next time, along the lines of *'Network Marketing... What I Wish I'd Known Five Years Ago,'* would have been of positive value and may well have attracted the interest of those new to network marketing.

Instead of this, however, she used the manuscript to vent her spleen on all those she - rightly or wrongly - believed had been responsible for her lack of success: the network marketing companies themselves, managers, uplines, downlines, customers - everybody. I'm sure getting this down on paper had some kind of cathartic effect, but it was of absolutely no interest or benefit to anyone else, and they certainly wouldn't be prepared to pay to read about it.

Sadly, this is not an isolated case. It seems that many people set out to write a book or manual on a subject close to their heart without stopping to consider whether enough people will share their enthusiasm to turn it into a viable commercial proposition.

I could give you dozens of examples, but suspect that at this point you're thinking: *"All very interesting, but what's this got to do with me?"* You'll be relieved to know that there is a purpose to this other than to complain about the problems of the publishing business. Now that would be ironic!

The key to success in publishing is the same as in any other business activity: the market must always come first. Yet few people seem to recognise the fact.

I regularly hear from people who have spent the last year developing and refining their 'thingummajig' which will do wonderful things. Just one problem though - they're not sure who will buy it, how much to charge, or how they're going to let people know it is available. Even worse, some of them have spent all their capital developing the product and they've got nothing left for marketing.

Whether you're writing a book, developing a new product, or considering marketing a product for someone else, set your own enthusiasms and interests to one side for a moment. Before you invest a single penny in cash, or a single calorie in effort, get three things very clear in your mind and then commit them to paper. Who (and how many) will want to buy this product? How much will they be prepared to pay for it? How can it be marketed to them profitably?

For most of us, this 'market first' approach is not a natural sequence of events, but is absolutely essential. Ventures which are product led do succeed, but usually through good luck rather than judgment. Sir Clive Sinclair (a product-led entrepreneur if ever there was one) had luck on his side with his personal computer, but it deserted him with subsequent products, the marketing of which appeared to be something of an afterthought. By starting with the market and then working back to the product the chances of success are so much greater.

Only when you've carried out your market analysis to the best of your ability - unfortunately it's not an exact science - can you decide whether it's prudent to proceed. Carry out this process for every single project you undertake and the savings in time, money, effort and heartache will be substantial.

6. You Can't Please Everyone - So Don't Try!

Every year, the music media launches a series of polls to determine which groups and performers the public deem to be the best (and worst!) in a long list of categories. You might not be interested in who the fans think is 'Best Female Performer With a Moustache' (perhaps that's not a real category, but they do get fairly obscure), but something interesting emerges when you compare the lists of 'best' and 'worst' - in many cases, the same performers are named in both best and worst lists!

The Spice Girls were voted as 'best group' in many polls a few years ago, and yet were often voted 'worst group' in the same category. There's no doubt that they were a highly successful act in terms of records sold, money earned and general popularity. Yet enough people voted them 'worst group' for them to win that category too!

What this means is that the group provoke strong feelings both for and against. If I remember correctly, Chris Evans also had the distinction of topping the 'best' and 'worst' sections in his particular category, for much the same reason. There's a valuable lesson to be learned here, whatever money making activity you're involved in.

I know that people looking for a business or money making project to start are hypersensitive to the opinions and reactions of others. This is understandable. After all, it's new to them, and whenever we try something new we tend to seek out the opinion and approval of others. How can we be confident about something we have little or no experience of? You'll recall that we looked at this in the section on choosing your advisors carefully.

A few negative comments are translated into "Nobody is interested in (or would pay much for) that product or service." Only unquestioned acceptance by at least 50 per cent of people is deemed grounds for proceeding. Big mistake!

The majority of people will not be interested in your product or service, no matter what it is you're selling. And here's something else - the more expensive, exclusive or specialist it is, the less people will be interested in it. But that doesn't matter at all. What you need to identify and concentrate on is the people who are interested.

Look at it this way. If you have a local population of 100,000 people, 95,000 of them may have absolutely no interest in your £100 product. They might even be antagonistic to it. They might hate it! But that leaves 5,000 who might be interested. Sell to ten per cent of them and you have a £50,000 business. Expand that out into adjacent population centres and you could quickly have your million pound business - and all from something which 95 per cent of the population have no interest in at all.

Many people starting out have the idea that you need a product or service which appeals to everyone and offends or upsets no-one. But strive for this, and in all likelihood you'll end up with a totally bland offering which doesn't upset anyone, but doesn't sell either! As an entrepreneur, you should be looking for niche products and services. You won't get far selling washing powder or cornflakes to the mass market. The big boys have got that sewn up.

Keep in mind that most people won't be interested in you or your business. But it really doesn't matter that some people positively hate what you do, because when that happens, there are others at the opposite end of the spectrum who will positively love it. Where there's hate generated, the opposite emotion is invariably generated elsewhere.

It's far better to be hated by 75 per cent of your potential market and loved by 25 per cent, than it is to be thought "sort of okay" by everyone. People pay hard-earned money for things they're excited about, and it's an all or nothing situation. People don't 'almost' spend their money. They either do or they don't.

Products and services which stir up both positive and negative emotions will generate sales. Products and services which leave people untouched emotionally generate few sales. And it's exactly the same situation with your advertising and promotions.

Create an advertisement which ruffles a few feathers, generates some phone calls and letters of complaint, and you can bet your life that it will be equally effective in generating sales. Create a bland advertisement which offends, upsets or 'turns off' nobody, and it won't provoke anyone into spending money with you either. So don't be afraid if your idea, product, service or promotion generates some hostility or negativity. Rejoice in it, because for every negative there is a positive. And a positive means someone spending money with you.

You can't please everyone, and you certainly don't need to. So don't try. Just ask the Spice Girls and Chris Evans!

7. Perception Is Everything

I don't know what life at your school was like, but at mine there was certainly a strict hierarchy to things. I'm not talking about the unimportant peripheral activities like performance in maths, english and science, but rather, the altogether more crucial matter of your ability to fight.

The 'rankings' were very clear to all, with the best three or four enjoying a level of status and respect which I'd wager they've never been able to match since. The 'cock of the school' was Stewart Rowe... a big fat lad, with a mean, ugly face - though I would have been reluctant to tell him that at the time! His position at the top of this particularly scabby tree went both unquestioned and unchallenged. And that's the interesting thing...

In five years, I never saw him have a single fight. Not once in all that time was he called upon to defend his position. Now that I think about it, none of the other 'top contenders' ever got into fights either. And yet their positions in the hierarchy never changed.

So what have these musings about my school days got to do with achieving your goal of stopping working and making a million pound instead? Well, the key force at work here is that of perception, and it's such a powerful force, that it creates it's own reality. Stewart Rowe had successfully created the perception in others that he was someone to be feared (which may, or may not have been true). That perception then took on a life of its own. Other people acted as if it were true, to the extent that nobody ever challenged the perception.

I'd even take that a stage further. If the perception had been challenged - if someone had taken a swing at him - the challenger would have been at a serious disadvantage, irrespective of any tangible factors that might affect the outcome. He would have been adversely affected by the perception.

Subconsciously, the challenger would have expected to take a good beating. This phenomenon was certainly evident in the early boxing career of Mike Tyson. Opponents were beaten before they had even got into the ring. But once the perception had been shattered by a brave opponent, subsequent challengers approached fights with Tyson in a much more positive manner, and fared far better as a result.

The bottom line is that you are what other people think you are. If you create a strong enough perception, it's very unlikely that it will ever be challenged, and if it is, then the psychological advantage will very much belong to you. Creating and achieving success relies very much on perception. The appearance of success and affluence often precedes the actuality. Witness the advice of Aristotle Onassis:

"Keep looking tanned, live in an elegant building (even if you're in the cellar) be seen in smart restaurants (even if you nurse one drink) and if you borrow, then borrow big."

Successful people want to deal with, and give business to, other successful people like themselves. Nobody wants to deal with the losers. Do you? If they haven't made a success of their lives, then just how are they going to make a success of providing you with the products and services that you need? Can you see why creating a perception of personal success should be of great importance to you? Can you see how it is that reality is more than likely to follow perception?

I've come a long way from those playground scraps, to World Championship Boxing, right through to international business success at the highest level - all within a few paragraphs - but the message throughout these examples remains the same - decide what it is that you most want to be, create the compelling perception that it's true, and the reality that you seek will be all the more likely to follow.

8. Positive 'Spin' Will Often Win

The winner of a competition I once ran reminded me that there's always more than one interpretation you can place on any given feature of a product or service. A slight change in emphasis can have a dramatic effect on whether this feature is seen as a drawback or a benefit.

Let's take, for example, a product you'll understand very well...You!

I regularly receive letters from people complaining that they're the 'wrong' age for the course of action they would like to embark upon, whether this is a new job or a business opportunity they'd like to take up. I get letters from 25 year-olds saying they're too young and letters from 50 year olds saying they're too old!

If I remember correctly, William Pitt the Younger was 26 years old when he became Prime Minister of Great Britain, and Ronald Reagan was over 70 when he first became President of the United States. Two more demanding roles it would be hard to find. Yet here we have men at opposite ends of the age spectrum defying any commonly held views about age.

Age, like many other personal and product characteristics, simply doesn't matter. What matters is the interpretation placed on it by the people we're trying to influence. And the person you need to convince above and before all others is yourself. If you're not convinced, how can you expect to convince anyone else? So, with age we have the benefits of experience, knowledge, maturity, diplomacy, responsibility and so on. With youth we would stress energy, adaptability, ambition and new ideas.

These are the interpretations we should use when trying to sell ourselves to a potential customer... or indeed, sell ourselves to ourselves as a potentially successful business person. Of course, it's all too easy to think only of the negative side of our situation, but what purpose does that serve for anyone? The positive side is equally valid in any case. When it comes to selling your product or service, this type of positive thinking can only stand you in good stead. For example:

• Your product may be second-hand, but say that it's re-conditioned, refurbished, or well cared-for and we create an altogether more favourable impression.

• Your product may be a little old fashioned. But isn't it also tried and tested, proven and established? Might it even be described as classic, traditional, or antique?

• Perhaps your product is expensive compared to the competition. But it's also excellent quality, exclusive, and value for money. It never pays to buy purely on price. The best is never cheap, is it?

• You might even have a poor quality product. But look how cheap it is. It's not the best, but it will do most jobs just as well as one costing twice as much. What a bargain! And it will wear out before you get fed up with it!

• Maybe we've discontinued the product. So it becomes an end of line bargain. It's a special purchase. Perfect stock at an imperfect price!

• Your product is a little small. Or should that be compact, easily managed, economical, will-fit-in-anywhere?

These are just a few ideas. For every potentially negative feature there is a positive benefit just waiting to be discovered. If you genuinely can't find one you need to enlist the help of someone who can, or improve your product - and that applies equally well if the product is you!

To return to the competition winner I mentioned in the opening to this section, he found a charity shop which didn't sell old clothes - they sold 'retro style clothing.' This is an altogether more enticing product. And Ronald Reagan didn't sell old age, he sold experience.

Work out the positive angle to every potentially negative aspect of your product or service, and you'll be one step closer to making your million.

9. Separate Baskets Are Essential

Most of the communications I receive from customers are positive and uplifting, but sometimes they carry within them the potential for disappointment and downfall later. Let me give you an example:

"Many thanks for the information on the xyz business. I've got started and it's going really well. It's just what I've been looking for all these years. At last my search is over. Thanks for all your help."

Nothing wrong with that, you might be thinking, and up to a point there isn't. That point comes where the writer says 'at last my search is over.' Looking for business and money making opportunities is not like some quest to find the holy grail, of which there is only one! It's an ongoing process.

Successful people - those that have stopped working and made many millions already - don't stop looking for new opportunities once they've become established in one sector. Once Richard Branson had established his mail order record business he didn't say "Great, that's me fixed up for life." He looked for new avenues to explore, as he did after setting up his record company, his airline, his financial services business and all the other divisions that now make up the Virgin empire.

Now please don't switch off here. I only use the example of Richard Branson because most people know at least a little bit about his business activities. I know that we're not all going to run multi million pound businesses, and most of us don't want to. We just want the best possible lifestyle and security for ourselves and our families, but the same principles and logic hold true.

The world is a rapidly changing place. A business or money making scheme which is working well today may well become unprofitable or unworkable next week as changes in technology, market tastes, competition or the law make it no longer viable. Other factors over which you have no control can have a dramatic effect on profitability. Just this morning, for example, I read yet another damaging report about the dangers of sunbeds. The effect on demand is not hard to calculate.

The old saying 'never put all your eggs in one basket' has always most readily applied to money making and personal finance, but it has never been more pertinent than it is today. The answer is to build up a portfolio of profit centres, preferably in divergent fields subject to different external influences. It is far better to have five money making businesses or projects each making £25,000 a year, than one making £125,000.

If one of your profit centres is hit by new competition, new legislation, world events or a shift in consumer tastes, you'll still have the others to fall back on. What this means, of course, is that your search for new opportunities must be ongoing - part of your daily routine.

By constantly adding new, albeit small, profit centres to your portfolio, you'll be making your position all the more secure. So when one of your profit centres falls by the wayside (and eventually they will) you'll have something to replace them.

10. Beating The Competition Is Easier Than You Think

When starting out in any business, it's easy to believe that others already operating that business - your competitors - have got it sussed. They really know how to bring in the customers and look after them, and you're going to have to do something pretty special on the advertising, promotional and customer service fronts to get a foothold.

This should be the case, but more often than not, it isn't. The marketing and customer service carried out by established businesses is often lacking in very basic areas.

This was brought home very clearly to me recently when I went in search of a new car (secondhand, but new to me). I knew the model and specification I was looking for and visited five main dealers. None had exactly what I wanted, but all took down my details and agreed to get back to me when they had something suitable. Then... silence!

A couple of weeks later I noticed that two of the dealers I had visited were running very expensive advertisements featuring cars exactly to the price and specification I'd given them. Yet neither had bothered to contact me.

You don't need to be a marketing expert to see the folly in this. And you can bet these people will be among those who complain that times are hard and people aren't spending any money. Needless to say, I didn't contact either dealer. If they couldn't be bothered to sell me a car I was desperate to buy, it did not bode well for the after sales service. I eventually bought from one of the other dealers, who kept in touch over a number of weeks until he found what I wanted.

Another recent purchase was a mountain bike. I went along to one of the most heavily advertised retailers, explained that I knew nothing at all about the subject, and threw myself at their mercy. The sales person was unable to explain what I would be getting at the various price levels, and any requests for an opinion given my circumstances was met with: "Well, it's up to you really." Despite having money in my pocket and being eager to buy, I left the shop empty handed and even more confused than when I'd gone in. Another sale lost, and someone else bemoaning what hard times we're having.

My cash was eventually spent with another retailer who took the time to find out exactly what I would be using the bike for, made a recommendation, and explained what I would be getting for my money, and why he didn't think I should spend any more or any less. What more did I need to know?

A couple of years ago, I visited the Homes and Gardens exhibition at the NEC in Birmingham. One of the exhibitors had an attractive garden fountain arrangement which I was interested in, and so I approached the company's representative. "Have you got a brochure?" I asked. "No, sorry," she said, and walked away.

That was it! Here was a company that had spent several thousand pounds to attend the exhibition who not only didn't have a brochure, but didn't even bother to take the names and addresses of people who were interested in their product. I can just imagine the Managing Director sitting back in his office with the sales figures on Monday morning, vowing never to attend any of these useless exhibitions again!

I could go on, but I don't think I need to. Unless you're very fortunate, I'm sure you've experienced something similar. The number of occasions in which it has felt like someone was actively trying to dissuade me from buying from them, are many and various.

For anyone starting out in a venture, there is a positive side to all this. You don't need to be a marketing genius to run rings around much of the established competition.

Simply know your product or service, help your customers to select what's best for them (without the hard sell), follow up on the people who express an interest in what you have to offer, and you'll be head and shoulders above much of the established competition.

11. Not Everyone Will Be Playing By The Same Rules

Just this morning I was playing I-Spy with my three year old daughter. Several rounds past normally, and then she came up with "something beginning with S." I tried several options without success, and had to admit defeat. "Suitcase!" she said triumphantly. "But I can't see a suit-case," I protested. "They're all in the cupboard!" "Well you should have looked," she said.

In all aspects of life, you need to be constantly aware that not everyone is going to play by the rules, and never is this more true than in business and money making activities. Let me give you a very simple and basic example. A little while ago, I had cause to dispose of a cheap bicycle bike via a small advertisement in the local free newspaper - the sort of thing most of us do from time to time. The asking price was £50.

The first phone call came before the ink was dry on the newspaper and the bike was sold within 30 minutes. For the next three days the phone never stopped ringing. I could easily have sold it ten times. I didn't sell ten of course, because I genuinely only had one, but it set me thinking...

What if I did have ten mountain bikes stocked up in the garage? They would be easy to obtain cheaply, either from trade warehouses or other private sellers (people invariably undervalue what they're selling - it's useless junk to them which they want out of the way) and I could quite easily have sold ten bikes - £500 worth, from an ad I placed for free!

So is there a catch? Of course there is - legal and moral restraints; rules.

Thanks to the Business Advertising Disclosure Order (1978) you're not allowed to masquerade as a private seller when trading. You could disclose yourself as a business person, but then you'd have to pay full rates for your advertising and the buyer might think they're not getting such a good deal - even though they may actually be getting a better one, since you're preparing your stock professionally.

There's also an ethical issue. Is it right that you mislead others for your own financial gain, even if they come to little or no harm by you doing so? So you're faced with a choice of being totally honest, or breaking the legal and moral rules a little to give yourself an edge.

Sadly this is a decision you may face time and time again, whatever businesses you become involved in. As entrepreneurs we are swamped by layer upon layer of rules, regulations and legislation, and new rules are being dreamed up every day. And then, of course, there's your moral code to consider as well. So what do you do about it? That's up to you. In the case of the law, you have to balance the possible penalties against the potential rewards. On the moral issue, you have to decide what you can personally live with. There's no other way. It's very personal.

What I can say for certain is that I don't believe there is a self made millionaire anywhere who hasn't bent, broken or blatantly disregarded a few legal and moral rules somewhere along the road to success, and frequently right at the beginning. Sorry if you don't like that, but it's the truth, and I hope that's what you expect from me.

The biography of Richard Branson, *Virgin King* (Harper Collins), revealed how the founder of the Virgin empire was forced to pay a penalty of £53,000 to Customs and Excise in the 1970s when 'a clumsy attempt at fraud' relating to the evasion of purchase tax was detected. One can only speculate as to whether this was an isolated case of stepping on the wrong side of the law or if any financial gain was made, but it does show that even the most 'ethical' of business people are prepared (and perhaps need) to sail close to the wind on occasion.

Another recent biography, of Michael Heseltine, former Chairman of the Board of Trade, revealed how early on in his property development career he would deliberately send out cheques to suppliers which were made out incorrectly, the intention being to delay payment and improve cash flow. I have no way of knowing how important this was to his fledgling business, but he did go on from modest beginnings to create a personal fortune estimated to be over £40 million.

Going back to my small advertisement example at the beginning of this section, one of Sir Alan Sugar's early ventures involved buying in a large quantity of black and white televisions, and then selling them via the local newspaper as 'unwanted gifts.' Later, when Sugar had set up Amstrad, and was having trouble getting the Comet chain to stock his amplifiers, he persuaded half a dozen friends and relatives to write to the company with an order for Amstrad amps. A few days later, a Comet representative rang him and placed an order for 100 amplifiers.

Arnold Schwarzenegger has admitted taking anabolic steroids in his bodybuilding career (not against the rules at the time incidentally but only because no-one knew about them - it certainly wasn't 'cricket'). Had he not done so he may not have become a champion, and therefore not had the opportunity to gain great acting and business success. It seems that for almost every success story there's a tale of legal or moral transgression to accompany it.

Please understand that I'm not here to encourage you to indulge in unethical or illegal practices. However, you bought this book because you want to stop working and make a million pounds instead. You want to hear the truth about wealth and success and how it's attained, not some sanitised version of how we'd all like it to be attained in an ideal world.

I often hear from people who would like to get started in a business but are afraid of contravening some minor regulation or stepping on someone else's toes. I can understand that, but my advice is always this:

Don't complain too loudly if you see others forging ahead by sailing a little closer to the wind than you're prepared to do. There will always be someone prepared to go that extra yard to achieve success... even if it means bending the rules.

The blunt message? If you don't want to bend the rules, and can't stand the thought of your competitors and contemporaries doing so, don't go into business at all. You will end up both disappointed and disillusioned.

To survive on a psychological level you need to be either flexible with regulations and ethical practice, or comfortable with the fact that others will undoubtedly be playing the game to a different set of rules.

12. Prices Are About Perception

I recently heard a taped interview with Ted Nicholas, reputedly the most successful self-published author in the world. In the early 1990s Ted sold his business for some astronomical sum and went into retirement with the idea of splitting his time between his two homes, one in Florida and the other overlooking Lake Geneva. The retirement lasted about three months!

Ted got bored and looked around for something interesting and fulfilling to do. He decided it would be a nice idea to run seminars for other entrepreneurs who wanted to maximise their marketing efforts. It was marketing skill which had made Ted his millions, and he wanted to share it. As I said, Ted had already sold his business for a very large sum. He certainly didn't need the money, so he decided to do the seminars for free.

You might think that by making such a fantastic offer he would be overrun with enthusiastic delegates. After all, here was the worlds best selling self-published author and marketing expert, prepared to give his time and expertise for free. Not so! The result was apathy, and the reason soon became apparent...

People value a product or service in relation to the amount of money they are asked to pay for it. So what's the value of a free seminar? Nothing! Ted learned from the experience. His seminars are now among the most expensive (and highly valued) in the world - anywhere between $3,000 and $10,000... and always sold out.

You see, the $10,000 price tag assigns a value to the seminar, and you'd think that any seminar costing that much must be extraordinary. What's more, when you've paid that much, you can bet you're going to pay attention and act on what you've learned. And so the whole process becomes a self-fulfilling success.

It's pretty well documented that most people who purchase a business franchise are successful, while most people who start a business independently, fail. I believe a large part of the reason for this is the price paid for the franchise. For £20,000 or so, it must be good, mustn't it? And with so much invested, you can bet you're going to do everything in your power to make it work.

Can you see how this links up with what I was saying earlier about perception and expectation? The price of a product or service creates a perception, which gives rise to an expectation. The perception and expectation arise out of the price assigned, and are independent of the intrinsic qualities of the product or service.

There's a lesson to be learned here, when setting a price for your product or service - whatever business you're in. The most obvious point is that a low price won't necessarily bring in more customers, and it might even bring in less. It all depends on the product/service - how the lower price affects the perception of its value, and whether this is important.

For example, a product primarily purchased as a gift for someone else may have its sales harmed by a lower price. Nobody likes to be seen as a cheapskate when buying presents! It's a similar situation with products and services where failure would have disastrous consequences. Anyone fancy a dirt cheap parachute? Or cut price cosmetic surgery? More likely you'll pay a higher price to be guaranteed the very best product or service.

On the other hand, a product purchased as a staple item (such as bread or milk) is likely to see enhanced sales as a result of a lower price. Nobody likes to pay much for items they need to buy, but don't necessarily want or desire. Only you are in a position to evaluate how the price you set for your product or service will be translated into a perception and expectation attached by the customer, and the effect this will have on sales.

The relationship between price, value and sales is far more complex than you might first imagine, and varies greatly between products and services. It's only by fully assessing what you're selling that you can make the most appropriate pricing decisions.

13. Momentum Brings the Big Rewards

Like a lot of cars these days, mine's got a fancy computer on it which tells you all sorts of useful information you never wanted to know.

One of the most disconcerting settings is the one which gives you an instant reading of the fuel consumption. Accelerate at anything above Reliant-Robin-with-the-handbrake-on pace, and the digital readout falls rapidly into single figures. It takes a surprising amount of energy (fuel) to take the car from standstill up to a reasonable speed.

But when you reach cruising speed, the readout is equally surprising. The energy required to keep the car at 80 mph is less than half that required to take it from 20mph to 30 mph. The fuel sapping part is the take-off and acceleration. Speed, in itself, does not require great amounts of energy to maintain.

Why? Because of the build up of momentum. It's all got something to do with Newton's laws of motion - a subject I would have been able to bore you on at length here, had I paid a little more attention in Physics lessons. No matter, you don't need to understand the science to appreciate the concept anyway. You see, the role of momentum isn't confined to the world of physics. It plays a huge part in business and money making activities too.

To get a venture up and running takes a great deal of effort at the outset. Just as the computer on your car shows a great deal of fuel being used while getting up to cruising speed, precisely the same effort to reward ratio is present in the early days of many businesses and money making enterprises. We put in a huge effort, and seem to get disproportionately little in return. And it's for exactly the same reason... we have yet to build momentum.

Once momentum in the business builds, we get the same benefits as we do in our car. The ratio between effort and reward shifts in our favour. We put in just a little more effort, and get a disproportionately high reward for it. We're not expending nearly so much energy, and yet the benefits we derive are so much greater.

Now I'm sure you've worked out that we don't have good old Isaac Newton to thank for this. It's a nice analogy, but the laws of physics don't really apply to business. There are however, a number of good reasons why momentum in business has the same effect. The twin keys to the growth in profits from any enterprise are higher sales and lower costs.

As your business gains momentum, customers you fought so hard to bring in 'through the door' for the first time, come back again without any effort on your part. Sometimes they'll order the same product or service again. Other times, you'll be able to sell them something else from your range. It all depends on the business you're in. Assuming you're supplying a good product or service, your early customers will tell friends and relatives about you, and these people will become customers, again without any effort on your part. And these people will tell their friends - and so on.

In the early days of any venture, you'll face a steep learning curve. You'll make mistakes, and sometimes they'll be costly. But as you gain experience, mistakes will become rarer and you'll find better ways to do things... ways which boost sales and slash costs.

One big advantage of momentum is economies of scale. The fixed costs associated with your business become spread over a far higher turnover, and because you're now dealing in bigger numbers, you're able to buy the things you need to run your business in larger volumes and at a lower unit price. The savings you make go straight to the bottom line.

As I'm sure you'll appreciate, I'm having to generalise a little here. I don't know the specifics of the money making projects you're going to be involved in, but these basic principles, and the benefits associated with getting momentum into your venture, apply to all business activities.

The point I'm trying to get over is this - in the early stages of building a business or working on a project, it will probably seems like the rewards you're getting don't justify the tremendous effort you're putting in. At times, you'll maybe look at people earning a regular wage with envy. Stay with it! In a relatively short time, you'll have momentum working in your favour rather than against you. I once had it explained this way - *"In the early days, you do a little work you don't get paid for. Later on you get paid for a lot of work which you don't do."* That's the power of momentum, and it's well worth sticking around for.

14. There's No Such Thing As A Negative Event

I'm sure you've heard the old saying "It's an ill wind that blows nobody any good." Like me though, you've probably not given it a great deal of thought, or pondered on how it might provide a basis for money making success.

I once heard a tape presentation by American success guru Dan Lee Dimke. He was talking about tornadoes - an ill wind if ever there was one - and how, despite them being an incredible destructive force, there is a positive side if you look hard enough.

Apparently there is a gentleman called Fujita who has made a career out of 'twisters.' He is a world expert, and the scale on which the severity of a tornado is measured carries his name. Thanks to tornadoes, Fujitas place in history is assured. Without them nobody would know who he was, and he may never have made his mark. Tornadoes have benefited others too. Numerous film makers, TV documentary teams, authors and photographers have enhanced both their professional reputations and bank balances as a result of work associated with killer winds.

When news of a tornado is reported in the press or on TV, great play is always made of the cost. It's always portrayed as a negative event, which is understandable. But one mans cost is another mans revenue. The cost of clearing up after a tornado doesn't disappear into the ether. It goes into the pockets of the enterprising individuals and companies who make it their business to deal with such matters. The following news treatment would be equally valid...

"Great news today from Jackson County, Texas, where a tornado ripping through several large towns has created a boom for construction

firms in the area. A spokesman for the local trade association estimated that $30 million of work would be coming the way of local building firms, and at least 1,000 short-term jobs will be created. Local hospitals also reported record business, with billings to insurance companies likely to approach a five year high."

I'm sure you realise that I'm using tornadoes as a euphemism for just about any "negative" event. The point is this: for any negative event there is always the other side of the coin - a positive side for someone. The task is to identify that positive side and capitalise on it.

Let's look at more examples. War and international conflict are universally regarded as negative. Yet for many - those involved in the production of armaments for example - war is good and peace is bad. It's the other side of the coin which we rarely look for.

Understandably, when my office was broken into, I wasn't in the mood to appreciate the positive side of the ever increasing crime figures in this country. However, the companies I subsequently paid to install an alarm system and roller shutter doors were probably better placed to do so.

Then there's economic recession, a prospect almost universally viewed as negative. Yet in any recession there are winners and losers. Reduced property, equipment and stock prices will provide an economic springboard to many new ventures in a recession.

Redundancy is also perceived to be a negative event. And yet an equally valid interpretation is to see it as an opportunity to make a fresh start, allowing time to find a new, more fulfilling path, and there may be a hefty redundancy payment to finance the search. Many people come out of redundancy with a far better paid, more fulfilling job than they lost, and with their redundancy payment still intact.

In addition to that there are organisations that benefit directly from redundancy, or the threat of it - recruitment consultants, outplacement consultants, re-training organisations, CV consultants, and dare I say it, writers and publishers of information which helps people to secure an independent income. There isn't a single 'negative' event which doesn't have a positive side - even death, as any undertaker or florist will testify.

The important thing is to identify the positive aspect to events and put yourself on the right side of the fence.

15. This Is As Good As It Gets

How do you feel about the following statements?

"The trade of advertising is now so near perfection that it is not easy to propose any improvement."

"Everything that can be invented has been invented."

I think most of us would at least see some truth there. Advertising is very sophisticated these days, even compared to 15 or 20 years ago. Surely we must be close to the limit of what can be done.

And the same could be said of invention and innovation. Over the past 100 years we've invented things to do practically everything man ever dreamed of, and a great deal more besides. In recent years the computer and digital revolution seems to have completed the picture. It certainly seems like there's little of any consequence left to be invented.

If you find yourself nodding in agreement with any of the above, consider the following...

The first statement, highlighting the perfection of the advertising business, was made by Samuel Johnson in 1759 - over 240 years ago. The second statement, bemoaning the downfall of invention, was made by Charles Duell, US Patent Office Commissioner in 1899 - over 100 years ago. In fact, his disillusionment caused him to resign from his job. Still, I'm sure he didn't miss much!

Here's the point. Pick any time in history and you will find that people felt that previous generations had it easier, that the opportunities were better and more plentiful, that it was so much more simple to make your mark in the world, that making money was much easier to do. If only we could have been around then. We'd have really made a go of it!

We have a word for this. We call it nostalgia. Fact is, when we look back at past opportunities we do so with the benefit of hindsight. When we're assessing the current openings available to us we have to do so using foresight. And that's considerably less reliable!

We can all look back a comparatively short time and say how much easier it was to make money in computers, software, mobile phones, or a host of other markets that were in their infancy at the time, than it is today. And we may well be right. But the people getting out there and actually doing it at the time didn't really know that for sure. It's only hindsight which adds the certainty. Foresight created the profit.

Here in the 21st Century, you can be sure that the new opportunities available, and the avenues for improving existing opportunities, are at least as plentiful as at any time in history. They're just not as obvious to you because you don't have the benefit of hindsight to guide you.

Don't fall into the nostalgia trap. In ten years time, these will be the "good old days" when getting rich was as easy as falling off a log. By then, of course, things won't be nearly so easy, and opportunities won't be nearly as plentiful. Except, of course, they will.

Remember, making money today is as easy as it's ever going to get. There's absolutely no logical reason for looking back, or delaying a moment longer.

CHAPTER 5

Making <u>Your</u> Million

I THINK IT WOULD be fair to say that no two people have ever made their fortune in exactly the same way, but one thing is fairly universal - they've all stopped working to do it. As I outlined in the introduction to this book, I mean that on two levels.

It's almost impossible to make a million selling your labour to an employer. Rates of pay are too low, and taxation levels too high for the great majority of people to accumulate wealth to any meaningful degree. You can no doubt point to exceptions..high flying city types, directors of major PLC's, Premiership footballers and the like. But does this apply to you? Is it ever going to apply to you? Me neither!

So you're going to have to stop working. Paid employment is never going to take you to your goal.

Whatever, you replace paid employment with (we'll come on to that in a little while) it's vitally important that you don't see that as work either. By making money from something you love...something you'd do for fun, even if there was no money to be made...you'll maximise your chances of a big financial success.

Most financially successful people carry on 'working' long after the financial necessity has past. The money isn't the important thing. It's the thrill of the activity, the deal or the challenge which drives them on. If you're to achieve your goal, you'll need to find something which makes you feel the same way. It's out there. You just haven't found it yet.

Paid employment is just one way of accumulating money, and as you've probably found, a highly ineffective one. There are three others I'd like to explore briefly, before looking in detail at what I believe to be the best.

1. Crime

Well it sort of fits the criteria. It doesn't involve work as such, if you're of the right mindset, I suppose it could be classed as enjoyable, and the rewards can be very high. There are a few drawbacks though.

Remember in the last chapter, I said it was okay to fail? Well fail here and you'll be locked up, during which time you make no money at all. This is an ongoing occupational hazard for anyone who chooses this path, and not one which many of us would care to live with.

In reality, very few criminals ever make any money. As always, you'll be able to point out the odd exception, but could you live like that? Always aware that a knock on the door could bring everything to an end?

There are plenty of perfectly legal ways of accumulating large sums of money, without breaking the law. Speak to anyone who has pursued a life of crime and they will invariably tell you that it was a mistake - that they wish they'd chosen a different path.

2. Gambling

"When I win the lottery..." You've heard that phrase often enough to know that this is the number one route by which most people intend to stop working and make a million pounds instead. No need for boring old books like this or taking positive action. Simply hand over a few pounds every Saturday (Lucky Dip is best - saves all that hard work picking numbers) and wait for those balls to come out of the machine. A fool-proof plan - if only it weren't for tedious old statistics.

The chances of an individual lottery line yielding a jackpot win are somewhere in the order of 14 million to one. To put that in perspective, these are longer odds than William Hills would quote you on Elvis Presley arriving by parachute during next year's FA Cup Final between

Carlisle and Accrington Stanley. Did I mention that Elvis would be wearing a tutu?

It's not going to happen. Nor are you going to win a million on the Football Pools or anywhere else. You're just not! The sooner you fully accept that, the sooner you'll put every last ounce of commitment into doing something realistic towards your goal. Just holding on to a little hope that it might happen is going to blunt your serious efforts.

Now, none of this means you can't make money from gambling. Approach gambling in a methodical and systematic way and it's perfectly possible to make a regular profit. But the statistics simply don't allow you to make the kind of money we're talking about here - unless you happen to be starting out with £10 million or so. Most successful professional gamblers clear between £20,000 and £40,000 a year - little more than a middle income job.

So does gambling have any part to play in your plan. I'd recommend just one thing, if you can afford it: Buy yourself some premium bonds. The top prize is a cool million, there are hundreds of other prizes every month, and you can get your 'stake' money back at any time. It's a no-risk opportunity, and one which might just see you reach your goal quicker than you thought possible. But let's not rely on it!

3. Working For Yourself

By this I mean engaging in an activity by which you sell your labour directly to end users, rather than through an employer. Examples of this would be a self employed plumber, independent solicitor, or freelance designer.

Although this type of activity is one step up from regular employment, it will rarely yield the million pound jackpot. You don't have to look too far to see the truth of this. Most small business people are not rich. Nothing like it. They enjoy many other advantages of course - no boss, work their own hours, control their own destiny... but rich? No.

If you're going to stop working and make a million pounds instead, it's essential that you set out in the right business in the first place. You can't guarantee that a particular business will make you rich, but set out in the wrong business and you can guarantee 100 per cent that it won't. In short, you have to give yourself a chance.

So what do I mean by the 'wrong' type of business for getting rich? The key to true business riches is the capacity for growth and expansion. Any business in which growth and expansion are impeded in some way is one in which you might make a good living, but will never make your fortune.

Purchase a business franchise and you'll probably make a comfortable living. But your capacity to grow and expand will be limited by the bounds of your franchise agreement. Wonder Pizza goes down a bomb in Littletown - fantastic! But you can't open up another branch in Bigtown. That's someone else's territory. So you won't get rich. If you want to get rich, don't buy a franchise.

Start a business which relies on your own labour and you won't get rich either. This is something which so many people miss.

Imagine you work as a plumber for someone else and decide to go it alone. It doesn't matter how good a plumber you are, you won't get rich. There's a top rate that people will pay for even the best plumbing work, and your earnings are restricted by the number of hours in the day. Multiply your hourly rate by about 12, and that's about as much as you can earn in a day. Stop working and the money stops coming in. This holds true for just about every business which relies on the business owner supplying the labour. There are only so many hours in the day, which creates a fixed limit on how much can be earned.

This is a vitally important point and so I want to emphasise it again - in order to make your million, the amount of money you make shouldn't be dependent on the amount of time you're able to put in personally. Even if you're in a highly skilled occupation, can charge your time out at £100 an hour, and manage to fill 40 hours a week with paid work, you'll earn no more than £120,000 a year after tax.

That's a nice salary, but it will take you a long time to accumulate your million - and you'll be shackled to your work for 40 hours a week. That's the thing about selling your labour. If you don't work, you don't get paid. In any event, are you confident that you can get someone to pay you £100 an hour, 40 hours a week, every week? Always?

Of course there are people who can charge hundreds of pounds an hour for their services, but they are few and far between. What I'm trying to do here, is to direct the average person - just like me - towards the money making activities which will yield them the greatest results. Those results will come from activities, the rewards from which are independent of the time you are able to devote to them. Or at least, activities which have the potential to be built into that in the future.

If getting rich is important to you, then it's important that you look at every prospective venture with a view to making it grow later on.

• *If you provide the initial labour, are the skills easily passed on to others you can trust?*

• *Would employees be able to do as good a job as you do yourself?*

• *Are you personally, central to the success of the business, or could you easily 'clone' your role elsewhere?*

• *Are there any legal restrictions on expansion (agency/franchise agreements etc)?*

• *Is the market large enough to warrant expansion?*

• *Is it possible to economically attract the large number of customers it will be necessary to find if the business is to become a fortune maker?*

These are questions you must ask yourself. If the answers aren't positive, it's unlikely that you have a business which will make you rich... ever! It may seem strange to be considering these factors before you've even started, but if your goal is to get rich, your first task is to choose a business which at least gives you a fighting chance. The last thing you want to do is spend several years working on a business which has no chance of taking you to your financial target.

Creating Your Own Money Machine

So we're agreed then? If you want to make a million, then crime is a non-starter, and barring a miracle, so is gambling. You're not going to do it working for someone else.

And as we've just seen, you're not necessarily going to get rich working for yourself either!

To stop working and make a million pounds instead, you're going to need to build your own personal money machine. This will take the form of one or more businesses or money making projects which provide an income, and ultimately wealth, far in excess of anything that can be achieved by any other means.

There are several characteristics I think you should be looking to build into your machine:

1. It should consist of multiple profit centres.

Remember, we discussed eggs and baskets earlier. It's important that your money machine can withstand a buffeting from any problems which might occur in one market sector.

2. You should be able to start small.

Do you want to borrow huge sums of money, and put your home and family security on the line to pursue your million pound dream? Thought not! Fortunately, there are enough low cost start opportunities around, that you never need do that.

3. It should be expandable.

Starting small is fine, but if you're to make big money, you're going to need a big machine. Some businesses work fine on a small level, but can't be scaled up, as we discussed in the last section. You don't want them in your machine.

4. It should be flexible.

The world is changing faster than ever before, and so are customer tastes and wants. Your machine needs to be able to react quickly to these changes. There's little point in having a machine dedicated to producing perfect 'watchamacallits' if 'watchamacallits' are yesterday's news.

5. Earnings should be independent of your time input.

This is very important. The number of hours that you can physically work is finite. The amount of money a customer will pay you for just one of those hours is limited. If your money making machine requires your constant input and attendance in order to to work properly, it will never get you to your goal.

The machine you build is going to be very personal to you. It will be a reflection of your own personality, experience, skills, education, interest, resources and effort. In the next chapter, I'm going to show you how to bring all this together, and create a machine which will generate a million pounds, and weather any storm the economy can throw at it.

I realise that from where you are now, this may seem like a daunting prospect - just as Everest seems a daunting prospect when examined from the foothills. Well, you're going to tackle it in exactly the same way - a single step at a time.

You've already taken the first important steps, by reading this far. The next step is to decide on your first profit centre - the business or money making project you're going to start in order to kick your money making machine into life.

Generating Your Own Personal Fortune Makers

The single major factor holding back those who wish to stop working and make a million pounds instead, is the lack of 'a good idea'. If you've been paying attention so far, you'll now know that the concept of a good idea (singular) is flawed, and that it's far better to look for a portfolio of ideas. However, you have to start somewhere, and that will be with one business or project. So what do people mean by 'a good idea'?

For 'good' you could substitute 'original.' People are usually looking for an original idea, which is a very rare thing and not necessarily a desirable or profitable one.

Take the example of Professor Rubik and his cube. This was certainly an original idea but he benefited very little from it. This was because he was immediately swamped by imitators on such a large scale that legal action was impossible. As the 'little guy' you can spend a small fortune and a lot of time developing an original idea and be powerless to protect it when it hits the market.

If you're looking for an idea which will become the 'next skateboard' you're going to be disappointed, and probably won't get into business at all. But this doesn't mean you should offer a 'me too' product or service just like everyone else. What it does mean is that you have to generate ideas based on existing knowledge which satisfy the needs of a particular market without attracting the type of competition with which you can't compete.

So how do you search for that first key idea? Start by asking yourself four key questions.

1. Have I got a special skill? It is easy to overlook skills and take them for granted.

For some reason I seem to know a lot of motor mechanics. It's probably got something to do with the state of the cars I drive, but that's another story. The thing I've noticed about car mechanics is that they all, almost without exception, hanker after doing something different.

They talk of 'giving up the tools' and doing something completely new with their lives.

I'm sure that car mechanics aren't alone in this, but they're as good an example as any of something we all suffer from from time to time: the 'grass is greener syndrome'. And I suppose they have a point. When you're up to your eyes in oil and grease, it's minus three degrees in the workshop and you've just slipped off a nut you were trying to loosen, scraping all the skin off your knuckles in the process, you may rightly reflect that there are more enjoyable ways of spending a Monday morning.

At such times it's all too easy to never want to see a motor car again... to think that this is the worst job in the world and to want to do anything other than work with things automotive.

I'll be surprised if you don't find some common ground with your own situation. So many of us, when we decide we've had enough of our job, want to get as far away from it as possible - to make a clean break and do something which has nothing to do with what we've done before. It can be a big mistake.

Let's stay with our miffed motor mechanic. He has skills, abilities and knowledge which he takes for granted, but which other people (like me) value highly. So he doesn't want to work for the local Ford dealers any more, but is it any good reason to go and sell double glazing? You may get to wear a suit and tie and keep your hands clean, but three months down the road that green grass will be starting to turn a nasty shade of brown as reality sets in.

There are problems our mechanic never considered, which are every bit as real as the grease, the cold and the scraped knuckles. What's more, he's starting from scratch. He's got no experience or knowledge to fall back on. The result? A new, environment, new problems but the same dissatisfaction.

So what should our man have done? The first place to start when looking for any new money making venture or business is your existing skills and experience. Our mechanic has intimate knowledge of the thing that forms the second largest item of expenditure (after a house) for most people - the motor car. That seems a pretty good place to start!

So he might not want to repair cars for Bogthorpe Ford Ltd, but what about starting a mobile repair service, or trading in cars, or valeting cars, or carrying out pre-purchase inspections, or selling car accessories, or breaking cars for spares, or writing a book on a particular aspect of car repair, or launching a newsletter for enthusiasts of a particular model, or teaching car maintenance at night school, or... you get the idea.

Associated with any job or skill there are limitless activities which open up completely new opportunities, while still taking advantage of hard earned knowledge and experience. Everyone should look at their own work based skills experience and knowledge, and explore possible spin-offs and derivatives, when looking for new ways to earn a living. Don't make the mistake of throwing the baby out with the bath water. Think of a business where you can use what you know in new, exciting and profitable ways. The most mundane of skills (driving for example) can be turned into a business opportunity, particularly when combined with a personal interest or previous experience.

Any skill can be used to provide a service, produce a product or teach. Remember, you don't have to be the best at something for it to be a skill. If you are only better than 50 per cent of the population then there are potentially 27 million people in Britain who could make use of your product, service or consultancy/teaching. Not a bad potential market!

Now that's not to say that you should never attempt anything new. In these days of rapidly changing markets and tastes, it's important that all promising avenues are explored, and that if possible, you build up a portfolio of money generating profit centres. In this way, you'll be in a position to ride out any downturns in any one area. But never neglect what you already have, and what you already know. It's the very best place to start.

2. Do I have a special interest?

Business ideas are often generated out of a personal interest. The individual who does this already has a head start because of his affinity with the topic. He already understand the needs of people who share this interest and are therefore in a tremendous position to capitalise on this.

Think about your own interests. For example, if you are a fisherman, how about manufacturing and selling flies? If you are a fitness fanatic, how about writing personalised training programmes, writing a weight loss book, or making a fitness video? There are bound to be needs associated with your interests which you can service.

For more years than I care to remember I've been a member of a small local gym. You'll note I said 'gym,' not health club, leisure club, fitness suite, or any of the other fancy establishments which have sprung up in recent years to cater for the middle aged, middle class and overweight.

No, this is an old fashioned gym - heavy weights, peeling paint and showers which leave you dirtier than when you went in! As you might expect, the clientele is mainly young and working class. More boots than brogues, more t-shirts than ties.

Hard to see this as a potential hotbed of entrepreneurial activity isn't it? There doesn't seem a great deal of scope for turning the mundane activity of heaving big weights around a 'sweat shop' into money making activity. And yet I've seen it done in a myriad of ways...

Mick looked around the gym at some of the flimsy equipment and decided that he could put his metalwork and welding skills to use to do a lot better. His company now not only supplies equipment to that gym, but to numerous others up and down the country and overseas.

Carl quickly realised that running a gym like this wouldn't be all that difficult, and so he went away and started his own place in a neighbouring town. Cleaner showers too by all accounts! Tony took note of the hundreds of pounds his fellow members were spending on nutritional supplements, and realised that they could be buying from him.

He approached a major supplier and took out an agency deal with them. He now sells several thousand pounds worth of supplements every year. Lee had always wanted to live and work in the USA. Armed with a 'new body' he sent his CV and photo off to a dozen gyms in southern California. He landed himself a well paid job as a gym instructor at one of the top establishments in Los Angeles.

Aside from these examples, who turned what they'd learned, seen or built into a full-time money maker, many others have developed part-time or second incomes from their interest...

Jamie became a professional strongman (ultimately winning the title The World's Strongest Man), making some money as well as travelling the world in competition. Martin became a professional wrestler, travelling throughout the UK and Europe, and no doubt dodging grannies' flailing handbags in every town. Simon became a part-time model and actor, appearing in numerous print advertisements and daytime TV shows. Mark went into the kissagram business. I think Tarzan was his speciality. Richard joined a stripping troupe. Seen The Full Monty? You get the idea! Oh yes, he also did a little 'gigolo' work on the side. Great stories, but not really suitable for here!

As you might expect, there have been countless others who have used their new-found brawn to earn extra money as nightclub doormen, debt collectors and bodyguards. Me? Well, lacking the inclination, looks, strength or courage to partake in any of the above, I used what I learned to earn money writing regular articles for bodybuilding magazines on a freelance basis. Not as exciting, but definitely safer!

Now here's the important thing - if there are so many ways to make money from such a mundane and low key interest, there simply must be as many ways to make money out of what you're interested in. And you're ideally placed to take advantage of the fact.

Take a little time to look at your spare time interests and activities from a money making perspective. You may be surprised to find that the money making opportunity you've been looking for has been right under your nose all along.

3. Do I have special experience?

Money making enterprises often develop out of past working experience and this can easily be overlooked. People often fail to see value in their experiences because they are commonplace - to them! However, they are frequently far from common to others.

Experiences don't necessarily have to be confined to work. For example, you may have moved house several times recently and are in the position to save people an expensive surveyors fee by identifying obvious faults (obvious to you that is). You may have bought several used cars, and using this experience could help others avoid a costly mistake. You may have travelled extensively and could provide an independent consultancy service to people going on holiday, informing them of the benefits and drawbacks of various resorts. Experience is valuable, and unique to you. Think very carefully about yours!

4. Do I have special possession?

Individuals often own high value items that are used infrequently, which could form the basis of a small business. Computer equipment, Video equipment, still cameras, vehicles, caravans, garages, garden sheds, power tools, sunbeds and musical instruments are just a few of the items which fall into this category. These items could all be used to make a start in a rental or service type business.

What To Do Next

Make separate lists of your skills, interests, experience and possessions. If you answer the above questions thoroughly then you will have four lists, from which you can start to obtain any number of possible combinations and business permutations.

For example, if one of your interests is cookery, one of your skills is speaking fluent French and one of your possessions is a word processor then this combination could lead you to think in terms of becoming a freelance translator of French cookery books!

This trite example shows that you may create many seemingly useless permutations, but illustrates the point. This method can help you hit upon one or more workable business ideas that are suitable - and perfectly viable - money making mediums you can make the most of.

Needs And Wants - The Basis Of All Good Money Making Ideas

All good money making ideas are based on a particular need or want. If people need or want something they will buy it, rent it, pay for someone to do it for them or find out about it. If they don't... they won't!

One of the best ways to find a profitable idea is to look out for unfulfilled needs and wants around you - things that people want but can't get, or things that annoy or worry them. This won't involve you in costly research - simply look at the things YOU want and can't get, as well as the things that annoy YOU about a particular product or service. The chances are that if they are a problem to you they will be a problem to other people too.

Make a list of products you would like to buy but can't - could you make or supply them? Next, make a list of services you find unsatisfactory - could you provide a better one? Also, make a list of things you worry about. Is there a product/service you can offer which will help to relieve it?

Research has shown there is a fairly universal 'hierarchy of worry' - the things that people fret about most of all. If you can help with any of these you will be entering a very lucrative market. These are:

1. Jobs/careers
2. Property/houses
3. Business
4. Family budgets
5. Memory
6. Health
7. Sex/attractiveness
8. World peace
9. Crime/burglary
10. Violence

Never overlook the obvious. There is a tendency to think: "That's too simple - somebody else must have thought of it." It is quite likely that even if somebody else has already thought of the idea, they have rejected it because... somebody else must have thought of it!

Another way of identifying a need, at least on a local basis, is to attend your local job centre and ask them which jobs they have a difficulty in filling. These represent an unsatisfied need and could provide a local money making opportunity.

Being Creative With Ideas

Ideas are everywhere. Look at what others are doing and ask yourself: "Could I do it cheaper or faster? Could I provide a better service?" Be flexible in how you view these ideas - they are not fixed entities but frameworks from which to develop your own angles and niches.

You need to break out of the 'normal' way of looking at things to find new and better routes. Searching for opportunities requires wide, creative thinking. Look at an idea from all directions and ask yourself the following questions about the product/service. This is quite an extensive list (though not exhaustive) and so not all questions will apply to every product or service...

What if it:

1. Was bigger/smaller/heavier/lighter
2. Was slower/faster
3. Was automatic
4. Was adjustable
5. Was easier to use
6. Was quieter/louder
7. Was stronger/wider/thinner
8. Was flexible
9. Was cheaper/more expensive
10. Had faster/slower delivery
11. Was turned upside down
12. Was more portable
13. Was combined with other products and services
14. Had more/less functions
15. Was better quality
16. Was poorer quality
17. Had a different size/style of packaging
18. Was disposable
19. Could be paid for in instalments
20. Was adapted for children

21. Was adapted for old people
22. Was marketed to men (female orientated product/service)
23. Was marketed to women (male orientated product)
24. Was sold in bulk
25. Was sold individually

Using this framework it's possible to generate thousands of permutations and spin offs from your ideas. Most of them, on their own, won't work as a business proposition, but will be invaluable in providing a stepping stone to 'the idea.'

The Power Of Lateral Thinking

Lateral thinking is the name to give to a different or unusual way of looking at ideas first written about by Edward de Bono and is useful in developing ideas.

When looking at ideas laterally it's important that you can temporarily dispense with logic. This sounds easy, but most people find it very difficult because their whole education has been based on logical thinking. Breaking away from this is hard and requires practice.

So how can lateral thinking be applied to searching for money-making ideas? Lateral thinking starts with a particular idea. It doesn't matter whether it is an existing idea that works, an existing idea that doesn't work, or an idea you have generated using the methods outlined previously.

The starting point for you is to say 'there must be another way of looking at this.' It is also where you must dispense with use of logic. Think of ways in which the idea can be changed, no matter how stupid or impractical they seem. The easiest way is to take a situation and reverse it. For example, a business idea might be to 'sell product X for money.' Lateral thinking could lead you to think 'give product X away for free, instead.'

You can see why logic needs to be suspended, as logical thinking will dampen your intuition and tell you that you will lose money doing this.

However, the value of a lateral thought is often not in itself, but in what it finally leads to. Therefore the proposition to give the product away free might lead to more practical ideas such as:

• *Give free samples away to influential, opinion-leading people in the community.*

• *Give a small free gift away with the product.*

• *Make a 'buy one get one free' offer.*

• *Promote product X to traders of higher value items for them to give away free with their product as a premium.*

• *Sell product X to charitable organisations who will distribute it free to the community.*

Therefore the original, impractical business idea can give rise to a number of workable ones if allowed to develop. To generate these ideas, it was necessary to take a sideways step by thinking laterally.

Lateral thinking is a very powerful tool for generating money making ideas and you'd do well to use it where possible in your own search for money making opportunities.

Unusual results often require unusual methods to achieve them. If you want to learn more, try reading one of Edward de Bono's books on the subject. Details can be found in the further reading section at the end of the book.

Ten Point Plan

1. Look at your skills.
2. Look at your interests.
3. Look at Your experience.
4. Look at your possessions.

5. Look for needs you can fill.
6. Make lists and permutate ideas.
7. Look at what other people are doing.
8. Be creative - ask "What if...?"
9. Apply, lateral thinking to ideas.
10. Take Action!

CHAPTER 6

Getting Down To The 'Nitty-Gritty'

THE SPECIFIC MONEY making machine you create in your quest to make your million, will arise out of the process explained in the last chapter. Whatever you come up with will be as individual as you are, because the combination of your skills, knowledge, circumstances, education, needs and preferences are unique.

However, the business (or businesses) you start will fall into one of a number of broad, recognised categories. The category of business you start is vitally important. You can virtually scupper any chances of making serious money right at the outset, simply by choosing the wrong type of business to start.

In the section on Creating Your Own Money Machine, I outlined some characteristics which should be present in the ideal venture for anyone with the serious intention of stopping work and making a million pounds instead:

1. You should be able to start small.
2. The venture should be expandable.
3. The venture should be flexible.
4. Earnings should not be directly related to your personal time input.

As a direct consequence of point No.4, the venture can become one of a series making up multiple profit centres for you. In the light of these criteria, we'll now look at the main fields in which you might be considering starting a business.

1. Manufacturing

There's no doubt that some of the biggest fortunes in history have been built in manufacturing. That doesn't stop this particular sector being a lousy choice for anyone aiming to stop work and make a million pounds instead.

There is a possible exception, and I'll come on to that shortly, but firstly, let me spell out the difficulties:

Manufacturing (making things) normally requires substantial investment. Starting small isn't really an option. Manufacturing operations are so advanced these days that you're probably going to need complex and expensive equipment, irrespective of what you're going to manufacture - just to get started. And then you'll be competing with established companies who are already benefiting from substantial economies of scale.

Manufacturing usually involves a significant labour input, and therein lies another problem. Minimum wage legislation in the UK means you can't possibly hope to compete on price with manufacturers in the Far East where rates of pay of well under £1 an hour are far from uncommon.

Certainly, a manufacturing operation is expandable, if you can raise the capital, but it isn't very flexible. It's going to cost you a lot of money to tool up to produce your 'whatchamacallit.' Let's assume for a moment that you're successful. You get your production right, keep your costs right down, and manage to produce your 'whatchamacallits' profitably.

But what are you going to do when people don't want 'whatchamacallits' any more, or someone else develops a technologically superior one? You're stuck with machinery and a work force set up to produce something that doesn't have a market any more. It's going to take a lot of time, effort and money to turn the situation round. You'll be starting from scratch again.

Your only hope of creating a manufacturing business success in the UK in the 21st Century is to look towards developing a unique, low volume, high quality, premium priced product - perhaps even personalised to the individual customer.

That way, you can sidestep some of the competition and cost issues which will almost certainly blight any attempts to go into generic volume manufacturing.

You can't sidestep the other disadvantages so easily though, and for that reason, I'd suggest you look very closely at all other money making avenues before going into manufacturing.

2. Retail

The retail business has also been responsible for some of the greatest fortunes ever created. Go back a century or more, and you find the likes of Jesse Boot, Franklyn Woolworth, Mr Marks and Mr Spencer creating businesses which were to continue to make massive profits for generations. Come more up to date and you find people like Anita Roddick, (Bodyshop) Charles Dunstone (Carphone Warehouse) and David Whelan (JJB Sports) doing the same thing.

The retail business has much to commend it. Depending on your idea, you can usually start fairly small, and investment is generally lower than in manufacturing. What's more, the business is expandable. If you hit on a retail concept that works it can be expanded either by extending the range of products sold, or duplicating the success of the outlet in other areas. It's usually possible - with proper staff training - to run a retail outlet at arms length. In this way, your profits are not directly related to the time you put in, a key requirement with any fortune maker.

On the down side, although investment is lower than in manufacturing, you're unlikely to get even the most modest retail premises leased, fitted out, staffed and stocked for anything less than a five figure sum. If you subsequently find that your retail concept doesn't work, much of this investment will have been wasted.

Retail businesses aren't amongst the most flexible either in that if your product type falls out of favour, or tastes change away from the specific niche you're serving, it's not so easy to quickly change direction. Stocks often have to be ordered seasons in advance, and a realisation that a mistake has been made or customer wants and tastes have changed will take a long time and a lot of money to put right.

I hope you understand that I'm having to generalise here. Not all retail businesses will share the same characteristics. A retail concept like Poundland for example solves the flexibility issue by stocking anything and everything - just so long as it costs a pound. That's a great concept by the way, but as an aside, you have to wonder about the quality of what the Poundland of 2020 will be selling!

If, after carrying out the exercise in the last chapter, you've come up with what you think is a winning idea for a retail business, by all means go for it. But don't decide just yet. The chances are, that if there's a retail opportunity, there's also something simpler, less risky, and potentially more lucrative you could do, based around the same idea.

In the appendix, I'm going to tell you about a retail business that retains many of the characteristics we're looking for - flexibility, expandability and relatively low start up cost. If I were going to start a retail business - this would be it!

3. Mail Order

Let me say straight away that there's no such thing as 'The Mail Order Business.' Mail order is a means of conducting business rather than a business in its own right. It's a means of marketing products, which could also be sold by other methods; retail for instance.

Mail order has a number of big advantages though, and we'll come on to those in a moment. First, let me make a further qualification - the term 'mail order' itself is a little outdated. Many businesses previously labelled mail order businesses, now take a large proportion of their orders via telephone, fax and e-mail. The thing that binds these businesses together is the concept of direct response - they approach customers directly via advertisements, direct mail, loose inserts, leaflets, TV and radio - and attempt to get a positive response directly from the customer.

Just bear in mind then, that when I talk about mail order, I'm referring to all businesses which attempt to illicit a response from customers directly, whatever form that response takes. Mail order has probably allowed more people to stop working and make a million pounds instead than practically any other.

Over many decades, mail order has consistently proved to be a genuine fortune maker. It has created rich and successful multi-millionaires out of thousands of people worldwide...some of them very quickly indeed. You may never have heard of mail order entrepreneurs like Melvyn Powers, Joe Sugarman, Ted Nicholas or Joe Karbo. Karbo, for example, went from virtual bankruptcy to a 'champagne and caviar' lifestyle in a matter of months, largely due to the success of a 'kitchen table' mail order business he set up.

Before you say "but that's in America, it can't happen here," prepare to be proved wrong. Mail order has been, and continues to be, a consistently successful business in this country too. You'll certainly have heard of some of the people and organisations who have made it big here. No matter whether you love or hate their mailings, the Readers Digest organisation is an excellent example of an incredibly successful mail order operation. The company's annual turnover now tops £160 million. The *Which?* organisation is another example you'll be readily familiar with.

Pick up a Sunday supplement and you can hardly fail to see the advertisements for Franklin Mint, Bradford Exchange and the like, who have made a fortune from selling 'collectables' by post. Even the high street names like Next, Littlewoods and W H Smith, now earn a significant proportion of their income from their mail order activities.

But it isn't just the big faceless companies who profit. Plenty of individuals owe their fortune to mail order. Peter Woods of Direct Line insurance became a multi millionaire by applying direct response techniques in the service sector. Sir Richard Branson owes a significant proportion of his wealth to the effective use of direct response techniques. In fact the entire Virgin empire was founded on the back of a humble mail order record business back in the 1970s. He's now estimated to be worth £800 million.

Now, of course, we're not all going to achieve this level of success. But there are literally hundreds of more modest examples of how individuals have started up a mail order based business in the UK with just a few pounds, and turned it into an excellent living for themselves.

Mail order fits perfectly into our criteria for an ideal money machine. It can be started small, with little or no investment, can be easily expanded, is flexible, and once up and running, can be left to run on autopilot. How do I know for sure? Well, at this point I have to declare a little vested interest.

You see, in 1990 I started a mail based business with a single advertisement costing £30. My total investment in the business was just £500, and I wasted most of that on stuff I didn't need - a fancy desk and chair, expensive stationery - that kind of thing. Well this year, my mail order sales will be in excess of £5 million, all built on that very first advertisement, and without injecting a single penny piece in capital. I'll give you some ideas for products which could form the basis of your mail order business in the appendix to the book.

If you're serious about starting a mail order business - and I think you should give it serious consideration - then my home study course on the subject may be of interest. You'll find details at the back of the book.

4. Agency & Middle Man Opportunities

Whenever I'm asked about ways to make a lot of money with little or no start up capital, one type of business venture always comes right up near the top of the list: the middleman opportunity.

The reason is simple. A third party has gone to the time, trouble and expense of creating a product. We've already seen in the section on manufacturing, how troublesome that can be. Someone else - somewhere - will pay money for it. By bringing these two parties together, the middleman earns a commission for him or herself without laying out any money or taking any risks.

These opportunities take many forms, but the job is always the same - introducing buyer to seller, in return for a percentage of the sale price.

Now here's the interesting thing. I'm sure you've worked this out for yourself. The bigger the sale, the bigger the commission. Yet the work involved in finding a buyer for goods costing £1 million is little different from that involved in finding a buyer for something costing £1,000.

So why not aim for the big sale?

Here's the really exciting thing. Practically every vendor of every product would be open to a middleman finding a buyer for him if approached in the right way. Why wouldn't he? After all, it costs a great deal of money to market a product. If someone comes along with a ready-made buyer who he will introduce in return for say, ten per cent of the order value, then the seller would be foolish not to accept the deal.

You can really let your imagination run riot with this. Opportunities to match buyers with sellers are all around you, if you tune yourself in to them. I was reminded of this recently when preparing an article for one of my newsletter publications. The story concerns an attempted middleman deal which didn't quite come to fruition, but it will hopefully open your mind to the breadth of opportunities which are out there.

A few years ago I was visiting a friend in New England. On a particularly wet and miserable day, he recommended we visit a place called the Yankee Candle Company, in a small historic town called Deerfield. Now I have to admit that I wasn't too keen on this, but my wife liked the idea so we went.

This place has to be seen to be believed. An enormous complex, tens of thousands of square feet, almost exclusively devoted to candles! Different sizes, different shapes, different colours, different scents. Want a personalised candle or one dedicated to your favourite football team? This is the place.

Dozens of tourist coaches were parked outside, and it was amazing to see ten-deep queues at the tills. Apparently they get two million visitors a year... to a candle shop! I took note, and nearly everyone was spending at least $70. They were doing a bomb.

Also on site was a car museum. My friend (who knew someone working for the company) informed me that this brought in a lot of people who otherwise wouldn't have come. I could see that - the men go and look at the cars while the women go and look at candles. All in all, it was a very impressive operation, and one that by all accounts had made the founder a very wealthy man starting from zero. Anyway, a couple of weeks after my trip, and with it still fresh in my mind, I happened to see an advertisement in the Businesses For Sale section of The Sunday Times. It read something like 'Entire contents of waxworks museum for sale... mainly historical characters... currently in historic UK city but easy to relocate.'

Can you see what I was thinking? Candles are made out of wax, so what a great tie-in! The Yankee Candle Company already had a car museum on site which made a profit while attracting more visitors, so why not add a waxworks museum which would appeal to children? I approached the company with the idea. To cut a long story short, they liked it, but eventually decided against. Why? I don't really know. Maybe it just wasn't the right time for them.

Okay, this didn't work out. But can you see how exciting this is? From nothing, I had created an opportunity to make a £15,000 commission. And what did it cost me? The time to make two phone calls and write two letters! Anybody could have done this without much effort or any capital. Similar opportunities are out there every day of the week, just waiting to be picked up. How long before one pays off, and what would you be losing by giving it a try?

You don't need a product, you don't need to carry any stock. Your product is anything you choose, and your market is anyone and everyone. There really are no limits to this. Why not start looking at high value products, properties and businesses you see for sale from a new perspective - as potential sources of lucrative commissions, rather than items to be purchased?

If you really want to stop working and make a million pounds instead, middle man opportunities are a great place to start. Capital requirements are zero, the opportunity is infinitely flexible, expandable, and because you get paid for spotting an opportunity rather than your time, this really should be in your portfolio of profit centres. In the appendix, I'll go into some detail on starting one type of middle-man type business.

5. Service Businesses

The service sector is huge and growing - an inevitable consequence of a mature economy. People already have all the basic things they need, but they have cash to spare and they're busy. Anyone who can come up with a service which will make their lives either easier or more comfortable, will find a ready market.

The range of potential services you could provide is so vast that it's hard to generalise. Window cleaners, advertising agents, hairdressers, solicitors, restauranteurs, car repairers, house sitters, wheelie bin cleaners... they're all in the service sector. Because the services you could provide vary so greatly, so does the suitability of the service in relation to the criteria outlined earlier. Capital requirements are variable. Some services are easily expandable and flexible - others are not.

By definition, offering a service involves doing something for someone else. If you're the person doing the 'doing,' and the service is dependent on that continuing, then you're selling your labour. In that case, you have a job - not a business - and your million pound goal will be no closer. Look at every service with a view to being able to clone your efforts, either by employing people or setting up agents or franchisees. If you can't do it, it's not the business for you.

In the appendix, I'm going to go into detail on one service base business you could start which has potential to be turned into a big earner for you. It's just one of hundreds you could profit from.

6. Trading Opportunities

I well remember the point in my childhood at which I knew beyond all doubt that becoming wealthy would be a piece of cake. It was when I heard the story about the father, his two sons and a chess board. There are many variations on the story, but it goes something like this:

A wealthy man was deciding how best to pass on his fortune to his two sons. He gathered his sons together and offered them a choice: they could either have £10,000 now in a lump sum, or they could receive just one penny now, but this would double in value for the next 64 days - one for each square on the chessboard. This meant that on day two they would receive two pence, four pence on day three, and so on.

The first son took the £10,000, wasted it on wine, women and song, and died broke. The second son hesitated, considered the situation and collected more money over the next 64 days than anyone could spend in a hundred life times. If you don't believe it, do the calculation for yourself.

What this story illustrates is the power of geometric progression. If you are able to double your money at each step, progress is both rapid and dramatic. While you're unlikely to have some benevolent relative to do the doubling for you as in our story, it can be achieved in business. Trading - buying and selling - is probably the most convincing example.

The concept is exciting, and on the face of it, infallible. Do you have £1 in your pocket? Of course you do. Do you think you could buy something with that £1 and sell it to someone else for £2? It would be easy wouldn't it? So, tomorrow you've got £2 to make a purchase which you sell for £4. Simple. Keep going like that for a mere three weeks and you'll become a millionaire.

Now I'm sure you haven't become quite as carried away with this as I did when I was eight years old. You'll have realised that while at the lower levels it will be fairly easy (anyone can buy a few pieces keenly at a car boot sale, clean them up, present them nicely and double the price), once you get into the thousands of pounds bracket the deals will become far more complex and need to be approached with care. And there will be other cost factors which erode the profits.

But whatever the level of business, the principles remain constant. Buy cheaply in bulk, split into more manageable quantities for resale, add value, and re-sell at 100 per cent mark up. At the lower end of the scale this might involve buying in a barrow load of golf balls recovered from a pond (buying in bulk), cleaning and sorting (adding value), shrink wrapping in packs of three (splitting) and re-selling. At the upper end of the scale it might involve buying in a container load of ex-catalogue stock for 12 per cent of its retail value, sorting and displaying it nicely in a shop, and putting on a massive mark-up while still selling at around 'half price.' Different levels of business, but identical principles.

Trading opportunities are very enticing for the aspiring millionaire. As we've already seen, they're expandable - find something that works on a small level, and then simply do more of it. It's flexible too. As a trader, you can deal in whatever products you choose. Unlike a manufacturer, you're not locked in to one product by your investment in plant and machinery. If the market shifts, you simply move on to something else. Most importantly of all, the size of your business and profits, are not directly linked to your own time input.

In the appendix, I'm going to look at one trading business you could set up for yourself, and expand into your fortune maker.

CHAPTER 7

How to Stop Working And Make A Million Pounds Instead - The Potted Version!

WHENEVER YOU READ a book like this, perhaps over a period of days, it's sometimes difficult to see the full picture. You know you've taken something from it, but are not really sure exactly what it is. That's how it is for me anyway.

Sometimes it takes a re-reading of the book to bring it all into focus, and you don't always have time for that. So with that in mind, I'd like to attempt to sum up what I've been trying to convey in the book in just a few hundred words. Hopefully it will act as an *aide memoire* to some of the more detailed information and ideas which preceded it.

Deep breath... Here goes!

• **It's okay to want to make a million for yourself.** It's morally and ethically acceptable, and by doing it you will create many benefits for others.

Making a million is an attainable goal. Over 100,000 people in the UK have already done it. When you do it yourself, you'll realise that it's a stepping stone - but you need to reach the stone first. Now is the very best time in the history of the universe, to do it.

• **To make your million though, you'll have to stop working first.** There are two reasons for this. Firstly, you will never accumulate large sums of money by selling your labour, and secondly, in order to put the effort necessary into 'something else,' it mustn't seem like work. You need to find something you love to do.

• **Before you can make your million, it's essential that you believe you can.** If you don't believe you can, you never will. Belief nearly always precedes acquisition. The more you expect, the more you'll achieve. People rarely, if ever, get more than they expect.

In all likelihood, you'll need to invest in yourself before you have all the tools in your armoury necessary to embark on the million pound journey. And then you'll have to re-invest as you progress. This is a very difficult stage because it involves making efforts disproportionate to rewards in the short term. Many people fall down at this hurdle.

• **You must take full responsibility for the outcome of any money making endeavours you undertake.** Accepting the possibility that someone else may ultimately be responsible for your destiny is an almost certain recipe for disaster and failure.

The hand you've been dealt in life, is the one you must play to the full. Certainly you can improve it by investing in yourself. That's positive and worthwhile. But bemoaning what you've been born and brought up with, and looking enviously at the hand dealt to others, is both negative and pointless. Somewhere within your hand are the seeds of a million pound fortune. You just need to find and nurture them.

• **Both at the beginning of your quest, and as you progress, various people will offer you opinions and advice.** Pay very close attention to the source of this advice and the underlying motivation behind it. Do these people really know what they're talking about? Do they have your best interests at heart?

Whatever ventures you undertake, they are unlikely to run smoothly. Everyone who has ever achieved anything of note has had to overcome obstacles and problems. They worked through them. You will not reach your million pound goal without a good degree of persistence and self discipline.

• **Along the way, you will experience failure.** This is normal. If you're not experiencing any failures, it's not a cause for celebration. It simply means you're not trying enough things.

Successful people think and act differently. So don't be afraid to be different - to go against the crowd. Average behaviour leads to average results, and this is inconsistent with attaining a million pound fortune.

• **Whatever venture or ventures you undertake, the most important consideration is the market.** Is there a market for what you wish to sell and can you reach it? Always consider this before anything else. Don't waste any time on ventures where this hasn't been established.

The way in which people view you and your product will be vitally important. You can create the perception which people have, and that perception takes on a reality of its own. You and your product are what people perceive them to be, and it's all under your control.

• **There's very little to fear from established competition in most fields.** The overall standard is very poor - as your own experience as a consumer and service user will probably testify - and you don't need to be a genius to compete. You just need to try that little bit harder.

Some of the people you're competing with will be operating to a different set of rules to you, and you need to be aware of this and be prepared to accept it or adapt to it. These are the only two choices. Complaining about it isn't a third!

• **The big rewards will come for you with momentum, and it's at that point that the relationship between effort and reward starts to work in your favour.** In the short term though, the work to reward ratio is unlikely to be favourable and you need to get through that.

One of the most important things you can do is to create multiple profit centres. That way, you are not reliant on one area of the market, and can ride out changes and variations in tastes, preferences and trends.

When deciding exactly what your profit centres are going to be, the following factors are important:

1. You should be able to start small and cheaply.
2. The venture should be expandable.
3. The venture should be flexible.
4. Earnings should not be directly related to time input.

By looking in detail at your skills, interests, abilities, possessions and experience, overlaying that with your new found knowledge about what people want, need and worry about, and then applying both creative and lateral thinking... you'll arrive at a unique personal list of potential projects and money making ventures.

Phew... a whole book in 890 words!

A FINAL WORD

THE NEXT 24 HOURS are crucial. Why? Because if you're ever going to take action as a result of what you've read so far, you will have to make a start in the next 24 hours.

It's your window of opportunity. Leave it for even two or three days, and the moment will have passed. The routines and demands of every day life will fully occupy your time and your thoughts. You will do nothing, and nothing will change.

So take action today - NOW! I'm certainly not talking about rushing into some venture or other without planning, but rather committing some of your ideas and thoughts to paper, asking for further information on things that interest you, researching what knowledge and skills might bring you closer to your goal. Once you've gathered your 'intelligence report,' you can start oiling the wheels to making your plans a reality.

The hardest thing about getting started is... well... getting started! However, once you're invested a little time and effort, the steps that follow become more and more automatic... in fact, part of your daily routine. That's why you need to take the very first step now. No excuses about work, domestic commitments or something good on TV. Do it now!

Good luck in whatever path you choose to take to stop working and make a million pounds instead. I look forward to hearing of your success, and perhaps publishing details of it in one of my newsletters one day soon.

APPENDIX

Four Hot Ideas If You're Stuck

IF YOU'VE FOLLOWED my suggestions in the final two chapters, you'll now be looking for ventures, projects and businesses which suit the particular mix of skills, interests, knowledge and interests you've identified - and it will probably be a venture from one of the following four categories:

1. Mail Order/Direct Response
2. Middle Man/Agent
3. Trading
4. Service

There are plentiful opportunities within each of these sectors which have all the characteristics necessary to allow you to stop working and make a million pounds instead. Just to recap, these characteristics are:

1. You should be able to start small.
2. It should be expandable.
3. It should be flexible.
4. Earnings should be independent of your time input or have the capacity to become so.

This combination of characteristics is necessary to:

a) Minimise your risk.

b) Maximise your earning potential.

c) Allow you to develop a portfolio of profit centres, simultaneously.

The whole point of this book has been to help you create your own personal money machine, and to give you the very best chance of turning it into a major fortune maker. But if you're anything like me, you'll appreciate a few ready made solutions - businesses and projects which fulfil all the relevant criteria which you could make a start with tomorrow. Would that interest you? Thought so!

So with that in mind, I've detailed five money making opportunities which could enable you to stop working and make a million pounds instead - or at least set you off along the right path for doing so. I've chosen one venture from each of the categories listed above... plus the unique retail opportunity I promised you.

Venture No.1:

Category: **Direct Response/Mail Order**

Venture: **Correspondence or home study course**

The terms 'home study course' and 'correspondence course' tend to be used interchangeably. The key element is distance learning. The student studies materials in his or her own home, that have been prepared and mailed by the course provider.

A typical course takes the form of a series of parts or lessons. The student works through the lessons in sequence, building up a knowledge of the subject as they go. There are usually tests and exercises to complete. Sometimes these are self-test exercises for the students to complete and mark themselves. Other times, they are submitted to the correspondence 'school' for marking and evaluation.

Home Study Courses are far from new. Go back 50 or 60 years and you will find home study courses on offer. Probably the most famous course of all time is *The Charles Atlas Bodybuilding Course*, first offered to the public in 1926. Look through any male orientated magazine today, and you will find advertisements for courses on the very same subject.

Although the world is constantly changing, people's underlying needs, hopes, fears and aspirations are not. That's why you see the same themes appearing in successful correspondence courses in the 21st century, as first appeared in the first half of the 20th century. It's an opportunity with continuing appeal which has stood the test of time.

Creating a correspondence course from scratch would make a good subject for... well... a correspondence course. Now there's an idea! This is a venture I have quite a lot of first hand experience of. At the time of writing, my company publish and run eight correspondence courses generating sales of around £1 million a year.

The courses my company offer, tend to be made up of 10-12 lessons and the student has the option of paying for each lesson individually, or paying for the whole course in advance to secure a discount. There are several reasons why a correspondence course makes an excellent direct response product:

1. The value is in the information rather than the substance (paper and ink) and so profit margins are high.
2. Markets are easy to reach because there is usually media targeted at the interest covered by your course.
3. The range of topics is almost infinite, so there's room for everyone.
4. Courses which fulfil underlying needs have enduring appeal.

Creating Your Course

If you've completed the exercise in 'Creating Your Own Personal Fortune Makers,' then I guarantee that you will have identified one or more topics on which you could base a correspondence course. There's an old saying that 'everyone has a book in them.' Well, I believe that everyone has a course in them. And what's more, if you do it right, it can be more lucrative than all but the most successful book.

Just to whet your appetite - my most successful course achieved sales of over £350,000 in a single year - and probably took up around six hours of my time each week.

I know that you have skills, experience and abilities which other people could benefit from, and which could be shaped and packaged into a course which would provide excellent value for your customers, and big profits for you. You just need to find out what it is. When deciding on a course to produce, always bear in mind the 'hierarchy of worry' I talked about earlier. You should aim to create a course which addresses one or more of these worries.

Generally speaking, any course aimed at making people wealthier, healthier, more attractive, or more powerful will have the greatest appeal.

Successful Home Study Courses

The course you create will be yours - a culmination of your knowledge skills and experience. There's little point in copying what someone else is doing - unless you can significantly improve upon it, or come up with a unique twist. But I'm sure, you'd like some inspiration. With that in mind, I've listed some successful home study course themes, together with my brief thoughts on why these subjects are so popular.

1. Bodybuilding/Physical Development. In our culture, being big and strong is something to be aspired to by young men. Rightly or wrongly, they feel it will make them more attractive to the opposite sex. And that's the underlying motivation.

2. Success With Girls. Attracting the opposite sex is a very basic human need. These courses home right in on that need.

3. Making More Money. Most people want more money. The fact that you're reading this book suggests that you're amongst them. Any course which helps people to make money will find an audience. I have several courses which fall into this category.

4. Successful Investing. People who have money want to make the most of it. Courses which help them to do that have always been popular.

5. Being More Healthy. Health is a major worry. Particularly in later life. Courses which guide people towards better health are becoming increasingly popular.

6. Writing. There are a lot of aspiring writers out there. Courses which guide people towards becoming published writers tend to do well. I have two courses for people who wish to become published writers in specific fields. There are many different strands in the writing field, and each could form the basis for a specific course.

7. Property. Property is a growing fascination - buying it, selling it, investing in it, renovating it, decorating it, styling it etc. Property related courses tap into this fascination. I have two property related courses in my portfolio.

8. Curiosity Subjects. The previous seven categories relate to courses which tap into one of the basic human needs or worries - money, career, health and sex. But there's a whole range of successful courses based around one of the most powerful of all emotions - curiosity. Sometimes a course can be successful, simply because people 'want to know'...they want to be in on some information which other people don't know about. Here's a group of subjects which have formed the basis of successful courses of this type:

• Fortune Telling and Prediction
• Private Investigation
• Hypnosis
• Memory Techniques
• Magic and Conjuring
• Handwriting Analysis
• Bodyguarding

Some More Ideas

While I think your course should fit somewhere into the aforementioned eight categories, there are other areas that you may wish to consider:

• Cooking/cuisine
• Drawing/Cartooning/Art
• Fashion and design
• Home Computing
• Genealogy
• Languages
• Music Business

- Photography and video
- Origami
- Calligraphy
- Cars and Driving

Don't forget the internet either. New people are going on line all the time, and courses designed to help people maximise their internet experience can be expected to find a ready market for many years to come.

Marketing Your Course

I can't give you a full course in marketing here, but I can give you some guidelines. By far the most common method used to promote and sell correspondence courses is the two-step system. This is very simple.

A small, low cost advertisement is placed in the appropriate media (newspapers, magazines and periodicals) in order to generate an enquiry about the course. The course provider then mails full information about the course to the enquirer, together with an invitation to enrol.

Once an enquiry generating advertisement has been proven to work - and assuming the follow up materials sent to the enquirer are generating enrolments - the advertisement can then be rolled out into other media. The keys to successful marketing are:

1. Keep a careful check on the source of all enquiries and enrolments.
2. Expand advertising that's working and cull advertising that isn't.
3. Follow up enquiries until it's uneconomic to continue.

Action Plan

I hope I've whetted your appetite a little. Get it right, and creating a correspondence course can make you a great deal of money. What's more, provided you take it a stage at a time, and follow my guidelines - most specifically with regard to monitoring the numbers closely - the risk of losing money, should the course not prove popular, is minimal.

Here's my ten step plan for developing, launching and profiting from your own correspondence course:

1. Decide on a course to publish
2. Prepare your course materials
3. Prepare your marketing materials
4. Place your test advertisements
5. Despatch sales materials
6. Fulfil enrolments received
7. Monitor and analyse results
8. Re-run advertising that works
9. Book more test advertisements
10. Go to No.5 and repeat!

Further Information

• *The Streetwise School of Copywriting Home Study Course.* Provides full training on writing sales materials for your products.

• *The Streetwise Mail Order Home Study Course.* Provides details on developing a marketing programme for your product.

Both courses are available from my company Streetwise Marketing. Full details available by telephoning or faxing us; Tel: 01709 820033; Fax: 01709 360611.

Bonus Correspondence Course Opportunity!

Here's another opportunity linked to home study and correspondence courses which I couldn't resist throwing in. I can't pretend that you'll make your million with this one, but it could be an excellent extra income opportunity for the right person.

Second-hand Correspondence Courses

Pick up any national newspaper and you will find dozens of advertisements for courses in any number of subjects. One of today's newspapers carries advertisements for courses in writing, painting, cartooning, improving your memory, speed reading, journalism, import/export, foreign languages, hypnotherapy, sports, nutrition, antique restoration, computing, counselling, practical English... the list is almost endless.

If you think about it, one of two things can happen when someone purchases one of these courses. Either the purchaser starts with enthusiasm, and then gives up before the end. Or they complete the course and learn everything it has to offer. It's a sad fact that the latter group will be in the minority. Unfortunately, most people fail to finish what they've started.

What this means is that there are an awful lot of courses sitting on bookshelves or hidden away in cupboards which are of no further value to the person who bought them. On the other side of the coin, there is great demand for courses in exactly the same subject. The fact that the schools and companies offering these courses continue to advertise year after year bears testimony to this. These courses are rarely cheap, often costing several hundred pounds.

So what we have here is a classic situation. A large pool of potential sellers who place a relatively low value on the product they have to sell, and an equally large pool of potential buyers, who place a high value on the product they'd like to buy. The potential for marrying these two groups together is obvious.

You could start by placing two advertisements, one a 'Wanted' ad for second-hand courses, and the other a 'For Sale' ad, offering courses for sale. From the 'Wanted' ad you will soon build up a catalogue of stock. Because the seller will, in all likelihood, have absolutely no further interest in the course, you will probably be able to get away with very low prices. For the reasons already indicated, buyers will provide you with a healthy profit while still obtaining the course at a significant discount on the retail price as new.

This business can be run exclusively by mail and you will be able to buy and sell on a national basis, using newspapers to locate your suppliers and buyers, and the Royal Mail to send and receive your stock.

Once you become established, you will probably find that your customers for, say, a writing course, will later be interested in your other courses. Some people simply like taking courses, irrespective of the subject. So you'll be able to grow through repeat business rather than relying on 'one-off' sales.

Other products may well fit in with this business, once under way. You may find, for example, that second-hand encyclopedia sets would fit in. They have some of the same characteristics as correspondence courses from a buying/resale perspective.

Where one group of people value what they own very little, and another group value that product very highly, an opportunity always exists for someone to intercede and take the balance of this variation in value as a profit. Here's your chance to do that now, in a very straightforward and simple mail based business which can be started without risk or great outlay.

Venture No.2:

Category: **Middleman**

Venture: **Import-Export Agency**

People are often put off the import/export field because the level of investment and expertise required is too great. However, you don't necessarily need experience in international trade procedures, knowledge of foreign languages and culture, or thousands of pounds in capital. The key is to set up as an agent rather than a principle.

It's possible to build a substantial cash generating business working from home with just a fax, a telephone, and an internet connection. The advantages of an import-export agency for anyone trying to stop working and make a million pounds instead are clear:

1. You can start small with virtually no capital outlay.

2. The business is flexible. Your product can be absolutely anything, and you have no long term commitment to any one product. If the market changes you can change with it.

3. The business is expandable. It's relatively easy to add new products to your portfolio.

4. Potential is limitless, and returns are not governed by your own time input. A million pound deal yielding you £100,000 will not necessarily take any more time than a £10,000 deal yielding £1,000.

Import agency

Working as an import agent is the most accessible route into the import/export field. Agents find buyers for their clients products and earn commission on sales. The agent acts as a go-between, finding a buyer for goods in the UK (or elsewhere) on behalf of the manufacturer in a different country. Dealing as an agent (as opposed to a principal, where you buy the goods in order to sell them on) has three major benefits:

1. It's low-risk, since you don't have to invest money in stock.

2. You don't have to deal with shipping arrangements and storage. You don't necessarily have to handle, or even see, the goods. You simply process payment with the buyer, take off your commission, then pass on shipment orders and balance of payment to the supplier.

3. You can earn between 2-15 per cent on each commission (five to ten per cent is average). You earn this on repeat orders as well as the initial order, so if the firm places a regular order you earn a regular income for little or no extra work.

The usual scenario is something like this. The agent discovers (perhaps by reading a trade journal, or trawling web sites) that a foreign manufacturer wishes to appoint an agent to sell their goods in the UK.

For an overseas company, it is often cheaper to appoint an agent to find a buyer, who will have experience and contacts in that country, than doing it themselves. The agent contacts the manufacturer to express interest, and obtain further information. If both parties are happy, a trade agreement is drawn up. The agents income comes from finding UK buyers for the firms products. On each order they take off their commission and pass on shipment details to the company, along with balance of payment.

Export Agency

Export agents source goods from their home country to sell abroad, rather than the other way around. In recent years the strength of the pound has made life difficult for exporters, making British goods relatively more expensive overseas. But certain products still sell well, bolstered by the UK's reputation for producing quality goods. If you can find a market where British goods are unobtainable, cheaper than the competition, or better than the competition, then massive profits can be made.

Import, Export Or Both?

The choice is yours. As I said earlier, the strong pound recently has made importing more attractive, making it possible to buy foreign goods relatively cheaply and profit by selling them in the UK. British products have a strong reputation abroad, however, particularly engineering products, so big money can still be made by selecting the right market for export.

Choosing A Country To Deal With

You can choose to trade with anyone you wish, but it's best to find a market, product and country you have prior experience of, perhaps through previous employment or personal interest. The list you made in Creating Your Own Personal Fortune Makers will be useful in helping you find suitable products, and markets. Country-wise, you might as well go for somewhere you like, have visited before, or have knowledge of. Otherwise, select somewhere with the same language and similar trading methods.

Language is important. If you speak no foreign languages it's wise to trade with English-speaking nations such as the USA, Canada, South Africa, Australia and Ireland for obvious reasons. However, your choice is far wider if you speak another language. If you speak Spanish, for example, you're ideally placed to deal with firms not only in Spain, but Spanish-speaking countries in South America and elsewhere.

Having contacts in a country gives you a head-start too, though it's far from essential. Think about who you know, where they live, and how they might be able to help you get started. Other practicalities that may influence your choice are the ease of travel, the strength of the currency and economy, and the (lack of) import and export regulations.

Choosing A Product

Again, let prior experience guide your choice of products to deal in. Let's say you used to manage a sports shop. Far better to make use of your experience and expertise by seeking to bring together manufacturers and retailers of sports goods, than getting involved in something you know little about.

Other important considerations include:

• **Price.** Is the product price competitive compared to other goods in your target market? Ideally your product should be slightly cheaper than the competition.

• **Demand.** Does potential demand make trade worthwhile? Is demand year-round or seasonal? How long might it remain in demand?

• **Competition.** Are there any similar products available in your chosen market?

• **Safety and legality.** Is the product reliable? Is it covered under warranty? Can it be repaired if necessary? Are there any trade barriers preventing its export/import? Does it conform to national safety standards? Toys from the the Far East, for example, are attractive to UK importers because of their low prices, but not all meet EU safety standards.

• **Suitability.** Is it appropriate for your target market? For example, electrical goods may be wired for the United States' 110v supply rather than the UK's 240v supply. Remember practical considerations. For example, foodstuffs may not be suitable unless they have a reasonably long shelf life. Bulky goods will be expensive to transport, so may also be unsuitable.

Above all, try to narrow down your choice of products early on. It makes the search for manufacturers and customers far easier, and it lessens the likelihood of having to drop a product after you've spent time, money and effort developing it and setting up contacts.

Taking time to search for the right product is vital. If it is particularly cheap and/or innovative you can develop a successful business in a short time.

Finding A Manufacturer

The next step is to find a manufacturer interested in dealing with you. Some agents like to approach companies 'on spec' by letter or in person, and this approach has its advantages. Some manufacturers may have never considered exporting their product until you put the idea to them. This way, you'll by-pass potential competition from other agents.

Firms who have identified the need for an agent, will often advertise in trade journals, and on the internet too. The upside here is that you know there's an opportunity. The down side is that you're going to be in competition with other agents for the product.

Once you find a suitable manufacturer, contact them by fax, phone, e-mail or letter to express your interest in finding an outlet for their goods. Ask for further details, including any available literature and samples, and information on any other products available, and suggested markets.

Making Important Checks

There are two main checks to make before you come to any agreement with the manufacturer:

1. Make sure you are allowed to import their products. Ring the Department of Trade and Industry (DTI), who will tell you whether that type of product carries import restrictions (because of import quotas for example, or because of laws regarding foodstuffs).

2. Investigate the suitability of the manufacturer and country. Attempt to find out if your potential trading partner is both ethical and financially stable by making enquiries via banks, business consultants, and credit agencies. Also investigate the country's trading practices, and whether any deal is likely to be affected by economic or political matters such as a dock strike or civil war.

Trade Agreements

If everything is in order, the profit levels are suitable, and both you and the company are happy to proceed with the deal, the next stage is to draw up a trade agreement.

As an agent, your contract won't make you liable for any transport costs, but there are additional considerations. It must detail your sales territory, the duration of the agreement, terms of renewal, the amount of commission and method of payment, along with who bears responsibility of advertising.

It's important to get exclusive trading rights, otherwise your buyer might start ordering direct from the supplier to save the amount of your commission. Also, make sure you have first refusal on renewal of the agreement - you don't want to lose your territory to someone else once you've spent time building up your contacts.

Finding Buyers

If you've done your job correctly, you'll already have a pretty good idea who your buyers are going to be before entering into an agreement with the manufacturer; in fact this is what will have prompted your interest in acting as an agent in the first place.

Remember what I said earlier in the book? The market must always come first.

Processing Orders And Payment

One of the most important parts of your trading arrangement is to determine the terms of payment. As an agent, this part of the job will be easy. When you find a buyer you simply process the order and arrange shipment direct from the manufacturer, not forgetting to take off your agents commission before sending on the balance of payment. Some firms may ask you to send on the whole payment before forwarding your commission.

Summary

Middle-man opportunities fulfil all the criteria you should be looking for. Acting as an import-export agent is just one possibility of many. Try giving a great deal of thought to ways in which you can bring buyers and sellers together to their mutual benefit. It will be time well spent.

Further Information

The following can be contacted for further information and assistance. Many publish help guides and leaflets. Some will allow you access to trade journals, and will hold details on trade fairs and delegations.

• British Chambers of Commerce, Manning House, 22 Carlisle Place, London SW1P 1JA; Tel: 0207 565 2000; WWW: www.britishchambers.org.uk.

• British Importers Confederation, Rooms 301-315, 3rd Floor Kemp House, 152-160 City Road, London EC1V 2NP; Tel: 0891 200250 (information line).

• British Exporters Association, Broadway House, Tothill Street, London SW1H 9NQ; Tel: 0207 222 5419; WWW: www.bexa.co.uk.

• Customs and Excise (HM), New Kings Beam House, 22 Upper Ground, London SE1 9PJ; WWW: www.hmce.gov.uk.

• Department of Trade and Industry, 1 Victoria Street, London SW1H 0ET; 0207 215 5000; WWW: www.dti.gov.uk.

• DTI Services for Business; Tel: 0800 500200.

• Institute of Export, Export House, Minerva Business Park, Lynch Wood, Peterborough PE2 6FT; Tel: 01733 404400; Fax: 01733 404444; WWW: www.export.org.uk.

• London Chamber of Commerce and Industry, 33 Queen Street, London EC4R 1AP; Tel: 0171 248 4444.

Other sources of assistance and information include your local business library, Chambers of Commerce, Training and Enterprise Council, banks, the commercial sections of foreign embassies in the UK (importing) or UK embassies abroad (exporting), regional government offices.

Import/Export Courses

Further information on trading with international markets can be obtained from:

• Wade World Trade, 50 Burnhill Road, Beckenham, Kent BR3 3LA; Tel: 0208 663 3577; WWW: www.wadeworldtrade.com.

Venture No.3:

Category: **Service**

Venture: **Vehicle Sourcer**

Vehicle Sourcing is a low-cost alternative to car dealing, which takes advantage of our ongoing love affair with the motor car, and falls squarely within the criteria we've set for stopping work and making a million pounds instead. Since millions of pounds are spent on new and used vehicles every year, successful car dealerships make a massive profit. While it's a highly lucrative business, there are two drawbacks:

• Profits are generally offset by considerable investment in glossy showrooms, stock and support services. Even the Arthur Daleys of the business have to buy, or rent, a pitch.

• It can take many years of hard work to become fully established. Many car dealers start out by borrowing from the bank, and interest repayments can eat badly into profits. Others start by buying an old banger, preparing it for sale, and selling it on. They then invest their profit in a better car and repeat the whole process. It's not difficult to get started in that way, but the big profits take time and effort to achieve.

However, there's a way to get a slice of the cake relatively quickly, without having to invest any capital at all - by becoming a vehicle sourcer. A vehicle sourcer is essentially a middle-man; providing a service to the car buyer. We've discussed the benefits of middle man style opportunities at length.

The middle-man cleverly uses his contacts and knowledge without having to use his capital. In this case, he brings together the car buyer and car seller in a way that is mutually beneficial.

Here's how it works: A prospective customer contacts the vehicle sourcer with his requirements and budget. The sourcer then uses his network of contacts for that type of vehicle to secure the model required at the best possible price. As reward for his efforts the dealer pays the sourcer a commission - anything from £100 or so for an old banger up to £2,000 for a top-of-the-range luxury model. Alternatively, the sourcer may negotiate a fee in advance with the buyer for sourcing a great deal.

What are the advantages of using a vehicle sourcer when buying a car? Clients have much to gain by using a vehicle sourcer rather than buying a vehicle from a dealer:

• A vehicle sourcer will be more competitive on price. A customer may negotiate a ten per cent discount on their own, whereas a sourcer, using his knowledge and contacts, may be able to secure 15 per cent on the same model.

• A good sourcer goes out of his way to keep in contact with a prospective customer until he find what the customer wants. Car dealers are notoriously bad at following up customers.

• The vehicle sourcer is much more flexible because he carries no stock and isn't tied to one manufacturer. He can provide any car, new or used, that the client wants. Whether it's an F registered Porsche 911 in cobalt blue with air conditioning, or a brand new Ford Mondeo 1.6 four-door saloon, it makes no difference.

The Benefits To Your Customer

The car market has become increasingly complicated, and this shows no sign of abating. The range of makes, models and options available is mind-boggling - as is the number of places to buy a car, and ways to pay. Although the internet has opened up a myriad of information to the buyer, this has simply added to the confusion. People are confused. They need help.

People lead busy lives. They simply don't have the time to exhaustively investigate all these options and make an optimum decision. Remember they are starting from scratch, whereas a car sourcer will have all the relevant information and contacts easily to hand.

Getting the best deal on a car requires negotiation, and a significant proportion of the population are either uncomfortable with it or bad at it. Employing the services of a car sourcer, gets over that problem.

Running The Business

If you've been in the motor trade, perhaps as a salesman for a car dealership, you'll be able to move into vehicle sourcing relatively easily because of the contacts and knowledge you already have.

If you're a novice, on the other hand, it's best to find a specialist niche rather than cover the whole market. A typical scenario might see you specialising in the classic car market. You build contacts by visiting classic car shows and through classic car magazines. Other areas of specialisation might be sports cars, a particular marque (Ferrari, Mercedes, Porsche and so on) or off-road vehicles. The more expensive the car, the more nervous the purchaser is likely to be about making a mistake, and the more likely they are to value the services of a car sourcer.

Marketing The Service

The best way to public is a vehicle sourcing service is to place ads in appropriate car magazines. With time, much of the business will come by way of personal recommendation and, of course, repeat business.

Start-up costs are minimal and the business can easily be run from home. You need a phone, answerphone, fax machine and e-mail connection. The biggest ongoing costs will be advertising and telephone bills. Any initial profit should be invested in a computer. This will enable you to establish a customer database and improve business efficiency.

Our love affair with the car shows no sign of waning. But increasingly we want real value for money. Vehicle sourcers are set to become much sought after in the future. The opportunity fits in with all the important criteria:

1. Start up costs are minimal and there's no stock to invest in.

2. The business is flexible. If one type of car isn't selling, simply move with the market.

3. The business is expandable. This would be a very easy business to franchise or set up as an agency network.

4. Earnings aren't directly related to time input. It's no more time consuming to source an expensive car than a cheap one, but the pay is better.

Vehicle Sourcing is just one example of the type of 'finding' service which is likely to become more popular as choice in most markets continues to grow, and the restrictions on peoples time increases.

New home sourcing, holiday home sourcing and antique sourcing are examples of other potential finding services which could find a ready market. Examine your knowledge, interest and experience lists to see if you can find others which might be right for you.

Venture No.4:

Category: **Trading**

Opportunity: **Trading In Consumer Goods**

This opportunity involves supplying consumer goods at discount prices. By consumer goods I mean appliances and equipment that are used in the home, every day of the week. This includes TVs, video recorders, hi-fis, kitchen appliances, computers, furniture and bicycles. In other words, items which everyone uses.

Here's why this opportunity is one you should consider:

1. You need very little capital. You can start by buying just one item and re-selling it.

2. You can start from home. You do not need any premises, nor any special equipment.

3. You can run the business part time, in evenings and weekends. (This is when most customers want to buy anyway). If you want to turn full time later on you can.

4. You do not need any special qualifications.

5. There is no hard selling. Consumer goods are already pre-sold by big manufacturers like Sony, JVC, Sharp etc. Customers need and want these goods. They will buy them from you because, since you do not have the overheads that shops have, your prices are much lower.

6. There is virtually no risk. If, after starting out in this business, you decide it is not for you, you can easily resell your stock using a small classified advertisement in your local paper and immediately recoup your outlay.

One Product Or A Whole Range?

When you first start it is a good idea to specialise in just one product line. This allows you to build up your expertise in one specific area and also makes your advertising more cost effective. However, as your business expands you should offer several product lines. This will enable you to develop lucrative repeat and cross-over sales. Is there a product which you have a particular affinity with because of your interests, experience or knowledge?

Buying Consumer Goods At Trade Prices

Here are the sources to consider:

1. Trade Warehouses. Trade warehouses stocking consumer goods exist in all areas of the UK and there are probably a good selection in a town or city near you. You can find them listed in magazines such as 'The Trader' and 'The Dealer' trade magazines.

2. Auctions. By and large, auctions are an excellent source of consumer goods. Their main advantage is that they are incredibly cheap, with goods often selling for as little as one half of one percent of their retail value.

The main disadvantage is that you cannot try or test the goods thoroughly, and they are not guaranteed. It is not possible to return them if they do not work. This involves an extra element of risk but you will find that the low price compensates for this.

3. Small Advertisements. One of the lesser known ways of buying your stock, but one which you will find very lucrative, is to place a small ad. for GOODS WANTED in your local paper. Perhaps you have seen these placed by established traders in your local papers?

This method is aimed at buying goods from members of the public and traders (mainly shopkeepers) who have items they wish to dispose of.

4. Catalogue Returns. Mail order catalogue companies deal in vast amounts of stock. Of this, a proportion is returned. Catalogue companies do not always place these items back into their stocks, but sell them to traders at a heavily discounted price. These are sold through auctions, trade warehouses and direct tender to the catalogue company.

Selling Via Small Advertisements

There are several possible methods of retailing your stock. However, the one I advise you to start with is selling using classified ads. The main advantage of classified ads is that they are cheap, but they still put your business before tens of thousands of buyers.

They also make it very easy to control your business since you can choose to place anything from one advert per week right up to several every day if you wish.

Nine Other Ways To Sell Profitably

Here are some other ways of selling. All of them work very well. Obviously, you don't have to use them all. Just choose the ones which suit you.

1. Selling to Past Customers and Their Friends
2. Window Cards and Posters
3. Leaflets
4. Direct Mail
5. Car Boot Sales
6. Garage Sale
7. One Day Sales (See Bonus Opportunity later)
8. Auctions
9. Developing a Network of Agents

An excellent way of expanding your business considerably, is to set up a network of self-employed agents in your area, or your region.

These people will offer and sell consumer goods in just the same ways that you do, except that you will supply them with the goods.

The advantage of this kind of operation is that you will multiply your sales several fold for very little extra work and time input once the network is set up. In effect, you have a group of enthusiastic and committed people working for you for nothing.

Trading consumer goods has all the hallmarks of the type of venture you should be looking for - low risk, low start up costs, flexibility, expandability, and no direct link between time and profit.

Further Information

How To Make £500 A Day Without A Job
Published by my company, Streetwise Marketing. Tel: 01709 820033 or Fax: 01709 360611.

Quick Bonus Opportunity:

Category: **Retail/Trading**

Opportunity: **One Day Super Sales**

You could combine opportunity No.4 with retail to create a new, and potentially very lucrative new opportunity! The One Day Super Sale offers you the chance to make big profits within a short space of time.

As I said earlier, retail opportunities often suffer from two drawbacks which render them less than perfect for our purpose here - which of course is to stop working and make a million pounds instead:

1. Start up capital is usually high, and it takes a long time to recover your investment.

2. The business is inflexible. If your product or product category falls out of favour, it's not easy to change.

This is a retail based opportunity which sidesteps both of these drawbacks. Become the Super Sale King! Here's the opportunity in a nutshell:

Hire a shop (or similar) for a day and hold a single product, single price sale. Your stock could be books, clothes, paintings, sports equipment, jewellery, lingerie, leather goods or whatever, all gathered from warehouses, closure sales and bankruptcies, and offered for sale at one single price, say £1.

You have various options as to where you hold your sales and what you sell. An empty shop is probably the cheapest venue, although you could hire a village hall, school or community centre, run a sale in a pub function room or car park, or any number of places.

It's worth matching the goods sold to the venue. For example, if you were selling sports goods then an obvious place to hold the sale would be a sports centre. As to what you sell, all the aforementioned goods are very profitable and can be obtained cheaply. You might also consider computer equipment, jeans and trainers, household goods and fancy gifts. Ex-catalogue goods are ideal, as they are often returned and sold off as slight seconds even though the fault is barely detectable - this is particularly the case with clothes.

Marketing Your Sale

The normal way of advertising such events is via advertisements in the local newspaper, although some of the bigger sales are even advertised on local radio and billboards. Having flyers printed is a cheaper option, as they can be handed out to people in the street locally to the sale, and dropped through letterboxes.

Super Sales have tremendous potential. Although some start-up capital is needed for stock, this can be turned around very quickly because you're going to sell most of your stock in one day. There are no long leases to worry about either; you'll only be renting for a day. And once you've gained some experience, you can expand the opportunity out 'hitting' a different town every week.

POST SCRIPT

I hope you enjoyed the book and are now brimming with ideas which will enable you to 'Stop Working And Make A Million Pounds Instead'.

If you have any comments on what you've read....good or bad....or suggestions for what additional information you would find useful, I'd be delighted to hear from you.

If you have an idea for a business or project which you'd like some feedback on, or a money making issue which you'd like an opinion on, then don't hesitate to get in touch via the address below. I can't promise to have all the answers, but I just might be able to help.

Good luck and best wishes with whatever you undertake.

John Harrison

c/o Streetwise Publications
Eden House, Genesis Park, Sheffield Road, Rotherham S60 1DX
Telephone: 01709 820033 Fax: 01709 360611

www.streetwisepublications.co.uk

FURTHER INFORMATION

I wouldn't be doing my job if I didn't take the opportunity to introduce some of the other courses, manuals and newsletters available from my company. To find out more you can visit our website at:

www.streetwisepublications.co.uk

Alternatively, if you would like a full product list sending in the post you can write to me at the address on the previous page.

For legal reasons we are obliged to state the following: